I MUST PRAY

A GUIDE TO A POWERFUL PRAYER LIFE

JOAN E. MURRAY

The Book cover was designed by, Woodson Creative Studio.

Joan Murray Ministries & Seeds Of Hope Worldwide Missions

26340 FM 1736

Waller, TX 77848

281-398-2501

PRAISE FOR I MUST PRAY

How do you write on a subject that can be both simple and complex, and make it appealing and digestible for both the beginner and the advanced? Well, Joan Murray has captured that technique in *I MUST Pray*. This book offers guidance for anyone just starting to connect with God, as well as encouragement for those who have battle scars from preserving in prayer. *I MUST Pray* is without a doubt a MUST read for every believer in Jesus Christ. It is truly evident the Holy Spirit spoke to Joan in preparing and writing this book. If your desire is to go from passive to powerful in your prayer life then plunge into *I MUST Pray*.

Marilyn Monmouth Williams, Co-Founder, Redeemed Chapel Christian Methodist Episcopal Church

Joan Murray teaches us in *I MUST Pray* how to face and overcome adversity through prayer. In order to be a conqueror in the battles that lie before us, we must pray. This book teaches us what to do when the enemy tries to distract us from what God has for us. It focuses on how to pray according to God's will, so we can find the sustaining power of God to take us through every trial or tribulation. In order to connect with God at a deeper level, we must first learn the proper way to approach Him. In *I MUST Pray*, Joan takes us on a journey through the Lord's prayer, as recorded in Matthew 6, and teaches us not only how to pray, but also gives powerful examples from the life of Jesus that will make our prayer life more effective and impactful. *I MUST Pray* is a perfect road map to a successful prayer life and a deeper relationship with the Father, Son, and Holy Spirit.

Zenola Lombard, Founder/President of Hair by Zenola & Tennessee Tailored Events

There is no greater privilege for anyone than being able to personally talk with and speak into the ears of Almighty God. If we, as children of God hope to speak with God as we spend eternity with Him, after our life on Earth is spent, we ought to start now. Prayer is a privileged access to the God of the universe. It was bought and paid for by the blood of His Son, Jesus. Prayer is available to all those who would freely receive Jesus as Lord. In this book, *I MUST Pray*, the author, Joan E. Murray explains why prayer means hope, help, relief, and power for everyone who spends quality time communing with God on a daily basis.

Rev. Emmanuel Okuidem, Redeemed Chapel

Within five thought-provoking chapters, author, Bible teacher, and prayer warrior Joan E. Murray provides a unique strategy for addressing our need for prayer. With many suggestions for a life of intercession, and continued connection with the Father, she provides a way for Christians to enjoy a more personal relationship with our Ever-Faithful God. *I MUST Pray* has increased my understanding of the necessity of finding time within my fast-paced, overwhelming lifestyle, to establish a vibrant, joyful, intimate, and sweet communion with the Father. This book focuses on many ways in which having a strong prayer life can allow for a consistent prayer pattern to emerge. We need to have our prayers heard and answered. Joan shares that "Prayers produce results!" They have everything to do with the soul's experience with God. As she guides us on this spiritual journey, we should be motivated to rejoice in having more frequent 'heart-to-heart' talks with our Father."

Theresa Smith Browne, Executive Director, Philia Works of Houston, Inc.

ACKNOWLEDGEMENTS

I thank the Lord Jesus Christ for His inspiration, leadership, and guidance in writing this book. I am always amazed by His inspiration as I write.

I thank my Board of Directors and the Joan Murray Ministries Team for their continued support, encouragement, and prayer each time I undertake another assignment to write the words the Lord gives me.

My sincere thanks to Pastors Jermaine and Ericka White, Zenola Lombard, Marilyn Monmouth Williams, Theresa Smith Browne, and Rev. Emmanuel Okuidem for their time and commitment to read and endorse this book.

Thanks to Julia Rigos and Rhonda Nalesnik, and the Xulon team. You have helped to make this book better because of your edits.

To my family and friends, thanks for your support and encouragement in the writing of this book.

A special thanks to Zenola Lombard for challenging me to write this book on prayer.

Thanks to the supporters of Joan Murray Ministries and Seeds of Hope Worldwide Missions for your support, prayers, and help as we take the gospel around the world.

CONTENTS

FOREWORD

When I met Joan Murray almost a decade ago, I immediately discerned the presence of God was a vital part of her life. Her conversation was effortlessly saturated with signs of one who maintains a strong lifestyle of prayer and one who studies the scriptures daily. I was mesmerized with her passion and joy as she taught a Bible study group; it was as if she allowed us to take a peek into the continuation of a private conversation she was having with our Heavenly Father.

As I began to engage in more conversations with Joan over the next few years, it became very evident she was not a pretentious person; she lived in the realm of prayer. It was at this time that I knew she had to become one of my mentors. What an awesome gift from God she was for a future pastor and leader in the body of Christ. Joan has not only provided encouragement and mentorship, but has played a vital role in praying and prophesying over the foundation of our church, members, and the vision of our ministries. We believe her prayers and support are a big part of why OneChurch has experienced ministry success over the past 5 years.

I believe Joan Murray is a rare gem in the kingdom of God and exudes the heart that the Apostle Paul had in mind when he charged us in 1 Thessalonians 5:17 to "pray without ceasing." Her lifestyle, leadership, and training give substantial credence for why the world should be an ear to the prophetic voice and words of "*I MUST Pray!*"

I MUST Pray is a must-read! Prepare yourself to be spiritually transformed, regenerated, and revolutionized from what you are about to learn. This book takes on one of the most essential yet challenging disciplines a Christian must develop head-on. It boldly confronts the topic of prayer by not only explaining *what* prayer does and the reasons *why* we must pray, but Joan Murray provides practical guidance on *how* we should pray.

Of all the many ways God could have chosen for humanity to communicate with him, He instituted prayer as His preferred channel. This is because prayer involves our innermost senses that require the participation of our soul. Joan makes this clear in a methodical approach that is biblically based. Each of the five chapters can be read as standalone units that are the building blocks to spiritual growth, or the entire book may serve as a key reference to supplement one's daily devotion.

As a founding pastor of a local church in Tampa, Florida, I began implementing some of Joan's concepts in our men's ministry.

For example, Joan explains how prayer harnesses the mind that can easily wander into illicit thoughts, but she provides realistic solutions for how we are to train our minds to think wholesomely through prayer. This knowledge is instantly applicable and I encourage you to grasp it as you read this book.

Moreover, Joan deals with the Christological and eschatological aspects of prayer in a manner that is easily understood. The bold title of this book, *I MUST Pray*, is strongly supported by Scriptural evidence of Jesus' teachings and personal life examples. Eschatologically speaking, one of the most poignant truths Joan reveals is God answers our prayers and we will see the answers to all of our prayers in eternity. This alone bolstered my perception of what occurs when I communicate with God; it even broadened my understanding of how prayer works.

As you read this book devotionally, I encourage you to pray before, during, and afterward. The principles Joan outlines are relevant, beneficial, and will produce noticeable results. You will begin to grow and think maturely about issues affecting your life, and your thoughts about prayer will shift from it being a required task or afterthought to a desired experience.

I learned a very valuable concept as I studied business administration in college. That is, the benefit of *economies of scale*. Simply put, the more items a company produces or sells, the less it costs to produce or sell those items. In other words, it is harder to do something sporadically than it is habitually. Thus, the more frequently you pray, the less effort it will take to maintain a renewed mindset and closer relationship with God. Grasping the wisdom contained in this book will tip the scales in your favor.

Jermaine White, Executive Pastor & Ericka White, Pastor OneChurch Tampa

INTRODUCTION

You may ask, 'Why pray'? The reasons we pray are as varied as the stars dotting the skies. Some of you have discovered that life is filled with hurt, pain, struggles, frustrations, and in some cases unending hardship. In the midst of these situations, prayer stabilizes us; eases our discomforts; frees our hearts; and comforts us. I have found prayer to be a place of solace in the midst of the storms; and have heard testimonies of how powerfully God intervened in the lives of people who prayed in the midst of tragedies. When they paused to pray, and to seek His face, God was there to restore peace and hope to their hearts during those times of devastation.

Jesus prayed often even though He was the Son of God. He needed to connect to God for peace and strength as He faced one difficult test after another. Although He was the Son of God, He still recognized His need for prayer. In the same way, we must also recognize our need for prayer.

Prayer helps you to rise above the raging storms of life, and in prayer you get a chance to anchor your hope and trust securely in the One who can rescue you.

There are some people who do not pray much because they don't know what to say. Others are unsure if prayer really makes a difference. Still others have tried praying and feel their prayers have remained unanswered. Let me encourage you, regardless of your challenges with prayer, God hears you and He will answer you. Do not abort or neglect this great gift, it is one of the greatest ways you can connect to God and find help in your time of need.

Listen, the God of this amazing universe wants an audience with you. He desires to spend one-on-one alone time with you so you can share your concerns with Him. In this place of intimacy, you will find He is not distant, but is a personal God and Father. You will also discover the depth of His love, devotion, and commitment towards you.

1 Thessalonians 5:16-18 tells us to pray without ceasing. Does that mean we stay on our knees all day praying without accomplishing much else? NO! It simply means for us to have an attitude of prayer; keeping our heart tuned into God at all times; pausing often to acknowledge Him as Lord; and expressing thanks simply because He is good. There are also times you can simply have a song in your heart that you lift to Him. All these are times of prayer because God is your ultimate focus.

In this book, *I MUST Pray*, you will find some answers as to why prayer is a must for your life. You will learn how often Jesus prayed, and discover how to get results as He did, when you pray. You will also find truths about why some prayers are unanswered. Finally, you will find sample prayers that can help you to develop a rich, full, and sustainable prayer life.

It is my hope you discover prayer to be an amazing adventure, and you will come to love this time of intimacy with the God-head. Get ready to have some divine encounters with the Father, Son, and Holy Spirit as you pray. I invite you to find your way to the feet of Jesus, and discover the healing and freedom prayer brings to your life.

Joan E. Murray

CALLED TO PRAY

"The opportunity to get away with God, when the pressures of life are overwhelming, is a priceless gift."

Have you ever prayed for God to move in your life and received the things for which you prayed? Many of us can testify to answered prayers. These instances do not necessarily mean we always received the answers the moment we prayed, but in God's perfect timing, our requests were granted. I have spent many years developing a prayer life and will be the first to admit that even though prayer is the foundation for a sound and wholesome Christian life, it is not often an easy task. Many people find it hard to be faithful and constant in their prayer life because the busyness of life has kept these believers from developing this greatest level of intimacy with God. In prayer, you and I can connect to God in a way that far transcends normal human interactions. When you make the decision to pray, to seek the face of God, you are connecting with the only One who has the power not only to answer you but to lift you out of every difficult situation.

Prayer, like praise, will lift the heavy load from your heart and eliminate your worries. The opportunity to get away with God, when the pressures of life are overwhelming, is a priceless gift. When I consider this wonderful gift of prayer, I am reminded God provided access to Himself so we can pour out our concerns and complaints to Him. The God of the universe wants a one-on-one audience with His children. He not only listens when you pray but responds with love and compassion.

In prayer, you get to share your most intimate needs with God. You also get to share the longings of your heart with Him and are then able to leave the burdens and cares at His feet. I call it 'shedding the weight'. You get to release any unnecessary weight you are carrying, and to unburden yourself into the care of God, your Father. God is able to handle everything that weighs you down.

Prayer requires a deep level of devotion to the One you serve. This devotion speaks of a deep love for God and complete dependency on His benevolence. You must be consistent in your prayer life; you cannot pray occasionally and expect the breakthroughs you seek. 1 Thessalonians 5:17 tells us to pray without ceasing. Does this mean you spend all day in prayer and therefore accomplish nothing else? No. It means you have an attitude of prayer and thankfulness throughout the day. As you do this, you will find God is always in your thoughts and His name is always on your lips. You are thinking of Him constantly, and even in the busyness of the day, you pause often to say thank you. Some people seem to always have a song in their hearts and on their lips. The moment they are unoccupied, they will usually begin to sing and commune with God. This, I believe, is developed out of the desire to stay in tune with Him.

I have prayed consistently for many years that God would always be on my mind and in my thoughts. I want Him to occupy every space in my heart and life. I have asked Him to be the first thought in my mind no matter how early or late I rise, as well as throughout the day. It takes training to ensure God is habitually in your thoughts, but you can do it. When you find yourself meditating on the wrong things, decide immediately to think about God instead, about His promises and His love for you. Train your mind to only think thoughts that are beneficial to your life and that will glorify and honor God. Prayer is where we are able to connect to God and find comfort and strength. It is a safe haven from the harassment of the enemy. In prayer, you tap into the peace of God that transcends human understanding; it is a place of solace.

I have found prayer to be a buffer in the storms of life. When I am worn out with stress or worries that try to overtake me, I find refuge in God. I say to Him, "Father, I don't know what to do but my eyes are on You," (2 Chronicles 20:12). Throughout the Bible we find many instances where God's people cried out to Him because they were in distress. King Jehoshaphat was one who poured his worries out to God. He was not ashamed to tell God he could not do anything without His help, and as a result, God fought for him and overthrew his enemies.

When faced with the threat of war, King Jehoshaphat

went immediately to God to inquire what he should do. He reminded God He was the God of their fathers. He told God if calamity came upon them that they would stand in His presence and cry out to Him in their distress, and then he boldly declared God would help and save them (2 Chronicles 20:9). He was not uncertain about the outcome of his prayer. He expected God to do something only God could do—answer him and bring deliverance. Because he prayed with boldness, confidence, and in faith, God responded to his requests. God wants you to pray with confidence and assurance that He will hear your request and move speedily to answer you.

We MUST pray because of what is happening both in our lives and around the world. Prayer is the key that will unlock the provisions of heaven in our lives. When disasters hit, people pray because they do not know what to do and they do not have the answers or the solutions, only God does. In your life, prayer is a MUST if you desire to nullify the attacks of the enemy. As we look at the number of lives lost in schools, theaters, on the streets, in families, and in other countries of the world, the only recourse we have is to petition the One who can change things. We MUST pray because we do not know what tomorrow holds. People are facing untold difficulties and their only solace and peace is found in prayer. When they connect to God in the midst of tragedies, He is able to bring comfort to their wounded souls. Many unexpected things will happen throughout our lives, so prayer is a MUST.

Prayer is a MUST if we realize it is the greatest safety net we have. Since we cannot see into the future, prayer helps avert some of the tragic events the enemy has staged for our destruction. Prayer activates heaven. Each time we pray God dispatches help. Hebrews 1:14 tells us God has assigned His angels to watch over us, the heirs of salvation. Their job is to protect and safeguard us; therefore, I believe when we pray and petition God, He dispatches angels to help us. It is evident that angels are God's agents in the earth, and throughout the Bible, we see their involvement in the affairs of men. In Daniel 9:17-23, Daniel began to pray and petition God for mercy for His people. While he was confessing his sins and the sins of the people, Gabriel, God's angel, arrived to give him a word. Daniel tells us he had seen Gabriel in an earlier vision so when he appeared in the natural, Daniel knew he was sent by God. Gabriel told Daniel as soon as he began to pray a word went out, and he was sent to deliver the message, the answer to Daniel's prayer. God also answers you the moment you pray. I believe one day we will have an opportunity to see all the results of our prayers. We will see how often, as a result of prayer, our lives were spared and how the enemy's attacks were prevented; and how what Satan meant for evil, God was able to turn for our good.

In the scriptures we find prayer was an essential part of the life of Jesus. He, the Son of God, with all power in His hands, recognized His need for prayer. He did not assume because He had an intimate father/son relationship with God there was no need to pray. He prayed because He loved God and valued His relationship with Him. He prayed because He needed God. He prayed because He needed strength. He prayed because He needed wisdom and guidance, and He prayed because He needed help. How much more should we pray that we will connect with the One who can help us in our need? Jesus communed with God constantly because He knew He would not succeed apart from Him. He set aside time in the midst of His assignment to ensure He was in fellowship with God and had the support of the heavenly host of angels when He needed them. Let's look at Matthew 26:50-54 so we can get a clear understanding of how God supports His own.

Jesus replied, "Do what you came for, friend." Then the men stepped forward, seized Jesus and arrested him. With that, one of Jesus' companions reached for his sword, drew it out and struck the servant of the high priest, cutting off his ear. "Put your sword back in its place," Jesus said to him, "for all who draw the sword will die by the sword. Do you think I cannot call on my Father, and he will at once put at my disposal more than twelve legions of angels? But how then would the Scriptures be fulfilled that say it must happen in this way?" Matthew 26:50-54 (NIV)

As you can see from this scripture angels are available to aid those who belong to God. Twelve legions meant Jesus had access to approximately 72,000 angels. The word "legion" was a military term taken from the Roman Army. A legion denoted at least 6,000 soldiers, even though the number could be higher. Jesus knew all He had to do was pray and God would release these angels to war on His behalf. God will do the same for us because we are His.

We MUST pray to activate the heavenly host to work on our behalf. Jesus prayed often. He continually sought an audience with God. As we review His passion for prayer, may we understand that without God's involvement in our affairs, we will not be successful. Throughout Matthew, Mark, Luke, and John, we find many prayers Jesus prayed. He did not go about His daily affairs without first consulting God; He knew the importance of connecting to the King of Heaven. Jesus understood God was His sustainer so He stayed close to Him, and as a result received strength as He fulfilled His earthly ministry. In chapter two we will look at some of Jesus' prayers and the results they produced in His life.

Not only do we get answers for ourselves in prayer, but at times God will give us answers or directions for those for whom we are praying. The Bible says those who have ears to hear let them hear what the Spirit of the Lord is saying. I believe the Spirit of the Lord is speaking many things into the hearts of believers but some of us are dull of hearing. I can honestly say I have been dull of hearing on many occasions. My hearing was dull because I did not spend enough time listening. It was dull because at times, when I did hear, I did not respond quickly in obedience. At other times I was dull of hearing as I could not believe what God was saying to me. I thought it was outside of what I could accomplish. My ears were also dull because of a sheer lack of trust in God. I lacked confidence He would do what I felt He was saying to me. Keep reading as I share a few examples with you.

God Can Use You Too

IN 2014 WE MET NETSAI, a 10-year-old girl who was in the hospital in Zimbabwe. She was in the hospital due to a bad car accident which left her with severe burns over 40% of her body; her mother had died in the accident.

When we initially met Netsai she appeared healthy and strong. The Holy Spirit, however, prompted me to ask why she was in the hospital since she appeared to be healthy. We were told she had been in hospital for over a year because her father was unable to pay the medical bills which were estimated at almost $5,000 USD. Again I was prompted by the Holy Spirit to gather more information about Netsai before leaving the hospital. The Holy Spirit then told me to, "Get her home for Christmas 2014." After returning to the USA, Seeds of Hope Worldwide Missions went on a fundraising campaign and we raised the funds to not only get her home for Christmas but to also pay for one year of schooling, all of her school clothes, and give her dad some money to help them with their needs.

When the hospital called Netsai's father and told him to come and pick her up, he did not believe them and thought they were trying to trick him into going to the hospital so they could arrest him for not paying his bills, and essentially abandoning her. The Pastor who worked with us to get her released had to call and assure the dad that this was not a trick and that God had indeed heard and answered his prayers. With tears of thankfulness and gratitude, he arrived at the hospital to hear the amazing story of what God had done. He could not believe God would intervene in his situation the way He had. God had taken a team of people on a mission trip, allowed us to visit that particular hospital, and then set the stage for me to meet this young girl and inquire about her welfare so He could reunite her with her family. To say the father and family were astounded and in utter disbelief is, to put it mildly, they discovered in a very real way God is involved with His children and cares about our suffering.

To say the hospital was amazed is an understatement! They had never in their existence seen anyone pay for a stranger's hospital bill. The story was printed in their local newspaper and reached the ears of the President of the country. God was glorified because He provided for this young girl and her family, and made it known He still cared about the needs of those who were poor and struggling. Here is another story of God's faithfulness.

On this same trip to Zimbabwe, we met a pastor and his wife who were struggling to hold on to their faith in God in the midst of their lack. This couple served God for many years but faced tremendous struggles due to the level of poverty in the country. After many years of praying and petitioning God, they were still unable to build a sanctuary and had only the frame of a building, with no walls, and a dirt floor. In addition, they were struggling with their membership and wondered if, after ten years of pastoring, they had missed God. Because of the severity of their struggles, the pastor felt he should quit the ministry, but God used his wife to convince him not to do that. She kept reassuring him God would grant their requests and give them a turnaround in their situation.

Some of us can identify with this pastor. We have prayed long and hard, and at times our requests are delayed and we are unsure whether we should continue to hope. If you are like me, you have probably cried, begged, and pleaded with God to give you those things you are praying for, at times to no avail. None of us fully understands why we do not readily receive the answers to our prayers. I can say emphatically, however, that if you will not stop praying and if you do not give up, God will reward you. When you are praying in alignment with God's will and His Word, God will respond. The dilemma we face is His timing is not ours and we must wait until He is ready to release what He has for us.

After the team and I served in several poor communities with this pastor and his wife working alongside us, we were invited to go and pray for their church and members. I felt a prompting from the Lord to accept his invitation but the enemy did his best to stop us from going. One of our drivers, after he finished his shift, neglected to give the other driver the keys to our van and it took a while to locate him and get the keys.

When we arrived at the church, we were astounded. It was approximately fifty degrees outside and what I saw was almost unbelievable even though I was seeing it with my own eyes. The church building consisted of a few poles in the ground and a roof. There were no walls only a dirt floor, yet the members were joyfully praying, praising, and petitioning God, as they waited for us. We were two hours later than planned because as I said, the enemy tried to stop us. As my team and I disembarked from the van, I understood why the pastor wanted to quit the ministry. He had prayed consistently for ten years to complete the building, with no results, and he was worn out.

The Lord instructed me to have the team and his members encircle the building as I prayed. The Lord prophesied He was going to provide for them and make them a beacon of hope in the community. After the prophetic word, I knew God would help them. I did not know how or who He would use but I had such an assurance He would; and yes, you got it, I was the 'who' God used. At no time during my prayer did I believe we were the answer God had sent to this man after his years of praying. Here is why, it had taken us a little over a year to raise funds for this mission trip. The trip was expensive, and I was worn out from all the fundraising efforts and just wanted to return home to the USA and rest. I was not looking for another assignment from the Lord. The next morning while praying the Lord clearly said to me, "Build the church." I said, "How Lord?" My hearing was not as dull this time. He said, "The same way you raised funds for the trip. Tell the churches that support your ministries, and sell raffle tickets." You guessed it! Within three months after returning to the USA we had raised the funds for the building, and a few months later their church was up and running. We firmly believe God will use it as a beacon of hope in the community.

I share these stories not to boast about what we have done as a ministry but to boast about the goodness of God. Even when we are slow to hear and even slower still to obey His instructions, God is still faithful. He does answer us when we pray. We can hear Him; and if we are willing and obedient, even when we do not understand how, He will indeed make a way for us.

God Hears Our Prayers

GOD HAS CALLED us to pray because prayer is vital not only to our personal survival but also to the survival of our society. Listen to what He says in 2 Chronicles 7:12-15, The Lord appeared to him at night and said: "I have heard your prayer and have chosen this place for myself as a temple of sacrifices. When I shut up the heavens so that there is no rain, or command locusts to devour the land or send a plague among my people, if my people, who are called by my name, will humble themselves and pray and seek my face and turn from their wicked ways, then will I hear from heaven and I will forgive their sin and will heal their land. Now my eyes will be open and my ears attentive to the prayers offered in this place."

Since prayer was taken out of our schools and other public organizations, we have suffered the consequences of that awful decision. The enemy has used this open door, this lack of prayer, to bring tragedy and devastation to many lives. We have seen the results of a lack of prayer in the number of deaths in public places; crime has risen dramatically; robberies have increased consistently from year to year; and peoples' lives have been cut short as murders have increased. Many innocent lives have been lost because without prayer to sustain a nation, without God, nations will crumble and fall. Prayer is the foundation, the thread that keeps a family, community, city, and nation together. When this most important part is removed, we soon find ourselves without the glue that holds all things together. God tells us if those of us who are called by His name will pray; He will hear and provide deliverance. To get answers to our prayers, we must connect to God. Let's examine what He is saying to us in this particular scripture.

In 2 Chronicles 7, King Solomon assembled the people for a festival to celebrate and dedicate the temple he had built for God. After it was over, he blessed the people and sent them home. At the conclusion of this time of prayer and dedication, the Lord appeared to Solomon. Many times the appearance of God in our lives is predicated on us doing the things that honor and please Him. Solomon pleased God so He visited him and gave him some great assurances. God told him He had heard his prayers. God is listening when we pray and He will always respond if we will be still and wait on Him. When God arrives, He always brings the answers we seek. The Lord told him when calamity strikes the people, if they would humble themselves, He would move in their midst.

Here is what I believe God told Solomon and is telling us. If we would remember Him; remember it is God who causes us to triumph; recognize we cannot accomplish anything in our own strength and might; and, if we would acknowledge that it is God who is our help and sustainer, then He would move in our midst. In humbling ourselves, we demonstrate our need for God. As we humbly pray to Him and turn from wrongdoing, from wickedness, then God will hear us and forgive us. God is saying if you will do this then He will move in your circumstances. We can also look at this scripture from another perspective that 'not only if' we obey but 'when' we obey God, He will bring healing to us and our land. When we humble ourselves, repent, and turn away from wrongdoing, God promises His eyes and ears will be open to hear us and He will pay attention to us. When God is paying attention to you it means He is available to respond to your every cry for help.

God has called us to pray because prayer is powerful and life-transforming. Prayer stops the enemy's destruction. Prayer causes God to act. Prayer reminds us we have no power of our own and we need God. Prayer helps us to see that without God in our lives and in our daily affairs, we will not succeed. Prayer brings peace and hope to our wounded souls. Prayer is the answer to the moral failures that are all around us. Will you pray? I MUST pray!

As I close this chapter let me ask the question that many of you may be asking. "Why does God take so long to answer my prayers?" I will explore some answers to this question in the upcoming chapters.

JESUS PRAYED

**"Listen, if the Son of God prayed as often as He did, you
and I have no option but to seek His face continually in
prayer."**

During the days of Jesus' life on earth, he offered
up prayers and petitions with fervent cries and
tears to the one who could save him from
death, and he was heard because of his reverent submission. Son though he was, he learned obedience from what
he suffered and, once made perfect, became the source of
eternal salvation for all who obey him and was designated
by God to be high priest in the order of Melchizedek
(*Hebrews 5:7-10 – NIV*).

Throughout His time on earth, Jesus prayed continually. He sought the face of God often and taught us how to
do the same. He stayed close to His Father through prayer.
From the scriptures, we see He spoke with God in the
morning, at mid-day, and night, and stayed in close fellowship and communion with Him. He was not limited by

time or manmade rules about which was the best time of day to pray. He understood prayer was a MUST at any time. From His example we find Jesus prayed without ceasing, and so can we. His connection with God was vital to His life and His assignment for mankind. Prayer kept Him steady as He journeyed toward each assignment that would culminate into His final assignment—death on the cross. Prayer sustained Him amid all the fiery trials He faced. When the Jewish leaders tried to trap Him so they could accuse Him of blasphemy, Jesus was able to withstand them because He had prayed. While He was in the Garden of Gethsemane prior to His crucifixion, He prayed. In each moment of agony, He prayed, and God strengthened Him.

You can see Jesus recognized His need for prayer. We must come to the same understanding that prayer is a need that MUST be fulfilled in order for us to have victory over life's challenges. Throughout the Gospels (Matthew, Mark, Luke, and John), you see the many times Jesus prayed. In this chapter, I want to explore some of His prayers so you can gain wisdom concerning what He prayed about. My goal is that you will learn how to pray and what to pray for so you will get the same results as Jesus.

Prayers That Avail Much

Luke 3:21-22 - When all the people were being baptized, Jesus was baptized too. And as he was praying, heaven was opened and the Holy Spirit descended on him in bodily form like a dove. And a voice came from heaven: "You are my Son, whom I love; with you I am well pleased."

WHILE JESUS WAS PRAYING, He experienced an 'open heaven' and connected with the Holy Spirit. In prayer, He heard God speak of His great love for Him and how pleased He was with Him. I am sure hearing these words brought joy and comfort to the heart of Jesus. God will also whisper His love and care for you when you pray.

LUKE 5:15-16 - Yet the news about him spread all the more, so that crowds of people came to hear him and to be healed of their sicknesses. But Jesus often withdrew to lonely places and prayed.

NOTICE, that Jesus prayed after healing the people. Could it be He prayed for the people to remain healed and that the enemy would not steal their healing? I have known of several instances where people received their healing and then the enemy came and stole it back from them. He was able to do this by convincing them that the healing did not really happen and they believed the lie. When they received the negative words it nullified their faith and caused them to doubt their healing. They began to feel the symptoms again but did not take authority over them, therefore, they ended up in the same condition as before and in some cases even worse conditions. In John 5:14, we see Jesus reconnecting with the man who was healed at the pool of Bethesda, with a warning, "Afterward Jesus found him in the temple, and said to him, "See, you have been made well. Sin no more, lest a worse thing come upon you."

LUKE 6:12-13 - One of those days Jesus went out to a mountainside to pray, and spent the night praying to God. When morning came, he called his disciples to him and chose twelve of them, whom he also designated apostles.

JESUS PRAYED all night before choosing the twelve disciples. For the Son of God to pray all night before making His choices, tells us that it was vital for Him to choose the ones assigned to Him by God. The only way to ensure He made the right choices was to earnestly seek the face of God for directions. We must also seek God for wisdom and direction concerning any and all decisions we make so that we do not miss His best for our lives.

LUKE 9:18 – Once when Jesus was praying in private and his disciples were with him, he asked them, "Who do the crowds say I am?"

JESUS PRAYED before asking the disciples who the people said He was. As a result of His prayer, Peter was given a revelation He was the Christ, the Son of the Living God. In our prayer time, we will get revelations from God and catch glimpses of the great things He wants to do through us.

LUKE 9:28-32 – About eight days after Jesus said this, he took Peter, John, and James with him and went up onto a mountain to pray. As he was praying, the appearance of his face changed, and his clothes became as bright as a flash of lightning. Two men, Moses and Elijah, appeared in glorious splendor, talking with Jesus. They spoke about his departure, which he was about to bring to fulfillment at Jerusalem. Peter and his companions were very sleepy, but when they became fully awake, they saw his glory and the two men standing with him.

THESE MEN SAW and experienced the glory of God and His Son. They also heard the voice of God as He praised His Son. In prayer, we will have divine encounters with God that will transform us and change the course of our destinies.

JOHN 6:11-12; Matthew 15:36 – Jesus then took the loaves, gave thanks, and distributed to those who were seated as much as they wanted. He did the same with the fish. When they had all had enough to eat, he said to his disciples, "Gather the pieces that are left over. Let nothing be wasted."

THERE ARE two instances where Jesus prayed and God multiplied the small amount of food He had to feed the people. Because He prayed, He was able to feed five thousand men plus women and children. Also in Matthew 15, after praying, Jesus fed four thousand men plus women and children with a meager supply of food. After giving thanks to God for what He had, even though the amounts were minuscule compared to the number of people surrounding Him, God increased the supply so drastically that they had many baskets full of food remaining.

We must realize that whatever we lack, God will supply it when we have thankful hearts. When we complain about our lack, we hinder the move of God in our lives. God has the amazing ability to take whatever little we have and to keep the supply coming until every need is met. You will find He did this throughout the Bible. He provided for the children of Israel, for the widows, and He will provide for you.

MATTHEW 14:22-23 – Immediately Jesus made the disciples get into the boat and go on ahead of him to the other side, while he dismissed the crowd. After he had dismissed them, he went up to a mountainside by himself to pray.

AFTER JESUS FINISHED ministering to the people, He sent the disciples ahead of Him as He took time out to pray. After completing His time of prayer, He walked on the water to connect with them while they were in the boat in the middle of the lake. His time of prayer fortified Him and allowed Him to do something totally contrary to nature. He defied gravity and the water sustained Him as He walked toward His disciples. From this example, I can infer that prayer gives us the power to accomplish what others may think is impossible.

When we pray, we are able to go beyond our limited understanding and abilities and accomplish great things. Prayer allows us to connect with the supernatural power of God. As we connect with Him everything becomes possible to us. Since Jesus made it a point to connect with God after a time of ministry and prayer, we must also understand our need to do the same. Once you have poured your heart out and given of yourself to helping others remember to take time to slip away with Jesus so you can be renewed, refreshed, and restored. These times of refreshing will ensure you are ready to handle the next challenge presented to you.

MARK 7:31-37 – Then Jesus left the vicinity of Tyre and went through Sidon, down to the Sea of Galilee and into the region of the Decapolis. There some people brought to him a man who was deaf and could hardly talk, and they begged Jesus to place his hand on him. After he took him aside, away from the crowd, Jesus put his fingers into the man's ears. Then he spit and touched the man's tongue. He looked up to heaven and with a deep sigh said to him, "Ephphatha!" (which means "Be opened!"). At this, the man's ears were opened, his tongue was loosened and he began to speak plainly. Jesus commanded them not to tell anyone. But the more he did so, the more they kept talking about it. People were over-whelmed with amazement. "He has done everything well," they said. "He even makes the deaf hear and the mute speak."

JESUS PRAYED while healing a deaf and dumb man. Some people brought the man to Jesus and begged Him to place His hands on him. It is important to involve others in your healing. Some people have great compassion for those who are struggling with the wounds they have been dealt. When we see them in their struggles, we have the answer—bring them to Jesus and ask Him to heal them. The people who brought this man to Jesus were not casual in their attitude toward him. They were involved with his needs and did not merely ask Jesus for help but begged Him to heal the man. They wanted him to experience the freedom that good health brings, and to prosper in all areas of life.

Jesus did something different in healing this man. He took him away from the crowd and did not allow the spectators to see this healing. He did not just command the healing but put His fingers in the man's ears, and then He spit and touched the man's tongue. Having done this, He looked up to heaven and with a heartfelt sigh, commanded his ears to be opened. We can conclude from this that Jesus knew the healing would require unusual measures, and because of this, He did not want to involve the people standing around. Had He involved them in this healing, it is possible that some might have been offended by His methods.

Although He is God, Jesus recognized that His Father is the ultimate Healer. He could have simply touched and healed the man but He gives us a reminder that all power to accomplish anything comes from God alone. His life was an example of always pointing people to the Father and giving honor to Him. The lesson to be learned from this is we should never believe we are the ones who heal or bring deliverance to those who are oppressed. We are only vessels God chooses to display His power. In Jesus' own words, John 14:10 "...but the Father who dwells in Me does the works." When we feel a little boastful or neglect to pray for God's intervention in human affairs, we will stumble and become like others whom God is unable to use. Remember, the Bible tells us pride goes before destruction and a haughty spirit before a fall (Proverbs 16:18). God is the One who is working in and through us at all times.

MATTHEW 11:25-26 - At that time Jesus said, "I praise you, Father, Lord of heaven and earth, because you have hidden these things from the wise and learned, and revealed them to little children. Yes, Father, for this was your good pleasure."

JESUS PRAYED for us and called us children. The first thing Jesus did before He prayed was to give praise to the Father. He gave thanks for who God is and what God does. We must do likewise. We must remember who we have the privilege of communing with. We have access to talk to the Creator of heaven and earth; therefore, we must pause often to express our thanks to God.

MATTHEW 11:28-30 – "Come to me, all you who are weary and burdened, and I will give you rest. Take my yoke upon you and learn from me, for I am gentle and humble in heart, and you will find rest for your souls. For my yoke is easy and my burden is light."

JESUS INVITES us to come to Him with our burdens and our weariness and to find rest in Him. I believe He is teaching us in this passage how to pray for our needs. He desires to exchange our heavy loads and burdens, with His abundant rest. Not only is He offering rest for our bodies but also for the turmoil in our souls. Consider the gift of peace God offers us. He wants us to enjoy our lives; therefore He has given us access to Himself through the channel of prayer, which is where we find ultimate peace. When we pray, there is such peace and comfort in His presence that we can rest in Him and in His promises to take care of us.

LUKE 10:1-3 – After this the Lord appointed seventy-two others and sent them two by two ahead of him to every town and place where he was about to go. He told them, "The harvest is plentiful, but the workers are few. Ask the Lord of the harvest, therefore, to send out workers into his harvest field. Go! I am sending you out like lambs among wolves."

JESUS SENT His seventy-two disciples ahead of Him into every town and place where He was to go and take the gospel. He told them to pray to the Lord of the harvest for laborers and sent them as messengers because the harvest was plentiful but there were not many workers. Their assignments were to heal the sick and tell the people the Kingdom of God was near. He told them anyone who listened to them was in essence listening to Him.

Each time we present Jesus to anyone who will listen, they are able to hear the truth about His greatness. We represent Him when we speak of His kingdom and showcase His gifts in the lives of those who are struggling. We are His hands and feet, and we get the privilege of telling others about the riches of His grace that has been poured out on us. Notice, Jesus sent them to every town and place where He would journey to minister. He sent them ahead to prepare the way. They were the trumpeters announcing through their work that something even greater would take place in their midst upon His arrival. When Jesus arrived, the people received Him more readily because they had already heard and seen what was possible simply by the use of His name. He sent the disciples ahead to prepare their hearts so they would willingly receive the deposit of wisdom He was about to impart to them.

After the seventy-two returned, they were excited about their experience and shared it with Jesus. They told Him even the demons submitted to them when they invoked His name. Jesus warned them not to get excited about demons being subjected to them but to get excited about what was important—their names were written in Heaven. Verse 21 tells us Jesus experienced joy after hearing the report, so He prayed thanking God for the revelations He gave them. Jesus is joyful when we obey Him and fulfill our assignments. God, the Father, shares this joy with His Son. Our efforts will produce a harvest for the Kingdom.

MATTHEW 19:13-15 – Then little children were brought to Jesus for him to place his hands on them and pray for them. But the disciples rebuked those who brought them. Jesus said, "Let the little children come to me, and do not hinder them, for the kingdom of heaven belongs to such as these." When he had placed his hands on them, he went on from there.

JESUS LOVES HIS CHILDREN. When the people brought their children for Him to pray over, the disciples tried to deter them assuming they were asking too much of Jesus. They did not realize Jesus wanted involvement even with the littlest members of His Kingdom. He told the disciples not to forbid the children from coming because the Kingdom of Heaven belonged to them. What was Jesus saying? What He said many times throughout the scriptures is that we must come to God as little children. We must come humbly, empty of our own desires, open to what He wants to do, and available to go where He leads. We should go to God as children who just want to spend time with Him, enjoying His presence. Just as Jesus blessed the children, He also wants to bless you.

LUKE 22:31-32 – Simon, Simon, Satan has asked to sift you as wheat. But I have prayed for you, Simon, that your faith may not fail. And when you have turned back, strengthen your brothers." But he replied, "Lord, I am ready to go with you to prison and to death."

WHEN THE ENEMY attempted to challenge and sift Peter's life like wheat, Jesus told Peter He had prayed for him that his faith would not fail during this period of testing. The devil wanted to destroy Peter's testimony and his love and devotion to God. The enemy was attempting to discredit him. Jesus, knowing the difficulty Peter would face did what He wants us to do on a regular basis—pray for one another. It is vital we not only pray for ourselves and our loved ones but also for those whom God has placed in our lives to lead us. You can see from this scripture that the devil wanted to nullify Peter's leadership. Remember, Peter was destined to lead the other disciples and to continue spreading the gospel when Jesus returned to heaven. The devil, therefore, was attempting to stop the spreading of the gospel by stopping the one designated to share it and disciple others.

We must pray for our pastors, leaders, and those whom God has given authority to lead and watch over us. Let's not assume that others are praying for them. We must do our part so we can prevent the plans of the enemy to destroy them. Like Jesus, pray for them so their faith will not fail and they will finish their assignments on earth. Pray without ceasing!

JOHN 12:27-28 – "Now my heart is troubled, and what shall I say? 'Father, save me from this hour'? No, it was for this very reason I came to this hour. Father, glorify your name! Then a voice came from heaven, "I have glorified it, and will glorify it again."

. . .

JESUS PRAYED ASKING the Father to glorify His name. In this scripture, Jesus tells the disciples the hour has come for the Son of Man to be glorified. He told them God would honor the ones who served Him and His servants would be with Him. Jesus also shared His heart was troubled and asked the Father to save Him from this hour; then He quickly said, "No, it was for this very reason I came to this hour." He came to this hour so God's name would be glorified. Jesus desired to glorify God's name and to make His name renowned on earth. He wanted people to know He was there not to promote Himself, but to promote and exalt God. May it also be our greatest desire to make God's name known wherever we go. Let it be your deepest desire to glorify God with your actions and attitude no matter what you face.

MATTHEW 26:26 – While they were eating, Jesus took bread, gave thanks and broke it, and gave it to his disciples, saying, "Take and eat; this is my body."

AS JESUS PREPARED to take the Lord's Supper with His disciples, and wash their feet, He offered a prayer to His Father. He took bread, gave thanks, broke it, and gave it to the disciples, saying, "Take and eat, this is my body." Then He took a cup, gave thanks, and offered it to them, saying, "Drink from it, all of you. This is my blood of the covenant, which is poured out for many for the forgiveness of sins." Jesus consistently showed us His need for the Father. Although He was God's Son, He operated with a great deal of humility, always involving the Father in everything He did.

The Son of God did not hesitate to serve the disciples. He was training both them and also us to serve others. His example of service is a demonstration of how God serves mankind. Jesus recognized that apart from God He was nothing, and consistently pointed us to the Father. He made it known His greatest desire was to honor, obey, and please God. His stellar example is for us to emulate Him. God is everything for the Believer!

JOHN 17:20-21 – My prayer is not for them alone. I pray also for those who will believe in me through their message, that all of them may be one, Father, just as you are in me and I am in you. May they also be in us so that the world may believe that you have sent me.

JESUS PRAYED FOR HIMSELF, His disciples, and all believers just before heading to Gethsemane. This is a significant prayer because it gives us an example of what we must also do. He shows us that in the midst of the severest difficulties, prayer is a MUST. We must pray for ourselves. Pray that God will deliver us from temptations, and evil influences and that we live lives that glorify Him. The Father wants us to present our needs to Him. The Bible says He is not slack concerning His promises (2 Peter 3:9). He will honor what He has spoken, and will come through on His promises regardless of what it looks like in the natural. Often we are deterred by what we see but God can do the impossible in our lives. Mark 10:27 tells us things may be impossible for men to perform but nothing is impossible for our God who is big enough to handle every hurdle you face. He carried Jesus through the horror of the cross and He will carry you too.

We must also pray for one another. I believe we should pray for others with the same level of passion, intensity, and desperation that we pray for ourselves. When we go through difficult times we often spend long hours seeking God for relief from these stressors. We petition, beg, plead, cry, and ask God for His intervention. In your need, you will do whatever it takes to connect to God to get relief or a breakthrough. If we would take that same level of emotion and desperation to God when someone else is facing devastating news such as sickness, loss, divorce, death, etc., this I believe will bring us closer to becoming more like Jesus.

Jesus prayed for Himself because He was about to face difficult times. In the difficulties, He would make decisions that would have eternal consequences for the human race. In Gethsemane, He would have to die to His own plans, hopes, and personal desires, to accomplish what His Father wanted—salvation for all mankind, so He prayed earnestly for Himself.

MATTHEW 26:36-38 – Then Jesus went with his disciples to a place called Gethsemane, and he said to them, "Sit here while I go over there and pray." He took Peter and the two sons of Zebedee along with him, and he began to be sorrowful and troubled. Then he said to them, "My soul is overwhelmed with sorrow to the point of death. Stay here and keep watch with me."

THE SCRIPTURE TELLS us when Jesus arrived in Gethsemane; He left His disciples as He went aside to pray. He told them His soul was sorrowful and troubled, and instructed them to keep watch while He went to talk to His Father. Jesus talked to God when He was feeling troubled. He sought hope from the only One who could encourage Him. He shared that His soul was overwhelmed with sorrow to the point of death. In these words, you can hear and feel the depth of His anguish. Jesus recognized He could not handle the turmoil in His soul by Himself; He could not carry this burden alone, He needed God. He teaches us there are situations that will arise in our lives that will traumatize us, but we have access to the Father to pour out our concerns and anguish to Him.

When Jesus considered the agony He would endure, He asked God if it was possible to remove the cup of suffering from Him. However, He then quickly surrendered His will to whatever the Father's will was for Him. He surrendered to the agony He would endure because He was doing it for His Father. Nothing was too difficult for Him to do in order to demonstrate His love and devotion to God.

His prayer in the Garden of Gethsemane that this cup would pass from Him was a two-fold prayer. The first part was a request for deliverance. God did not answer this prayer because our sinful condition would not allow Him to be free. There was no other way to free us but for Jesus to go to the cross. The second part of the prayer was a prayer of surrendering His will to God. The first Adam was defeated in the Garden of Eden, and the second Adam, Jesus, would regain our victory in the Garden of Gethsemane. Jesus restored the true meaning of what the Garden was intended to be, a place of blessings, peace, and prosperity. God had created a paradise for Adam and Eve in the Garden of Eden, but they lost it to the Devil. Jesus defeated the Devil in a garden, how fitting.

The prayers He prayed throughout His journey, and just prior to this situation, sustained Him when dealing with the agony of His soul. When we also pray in advance of whatever the enemy might throw at us, we will have sustaining power to see us through the rough times.

JOHN 17:1-26 (MSG) - Jesus said these things. Then, raising his eyes in prayer, he said: Father, it's time. Display the bright splendor of your Son so the Son in turn may show your bright splendor. You put him in charge of everything human so he might give real and eternal life to all in his charge. And this is the real and eternal life: That they know you, the one and only true God, and Jesus Christ, whom you sent. I glorified you on earth by completing down to the last detail what you assigned me to do. And now, Father, glorify me with your very own splendor, the very splendor I had in your presence before there was a world. I spelled out your character in detail to the men and women you gave me. They were yours in the first place; then you gave them to me, and they have now done what you said. They know now, beyond the shadow of a doubt, that everything you gave me is firsthand from you, for the message you gave me, I gave them; and they took it, and were convinced that I came from you. They believed that you sent me. I pray for them. I'm not praying for the God-rejecting world but for those you gave me, for they are yours by right. Everything mine is yours, and yours mine, and my life is on display in them. For I'm no longer going to be visible in the world; they'll continue in the world while I return to you. Holy Father, guard them as they pursue this life that you conferred as a gift through me, so they can be one heart and mind as we are one heart and mind. As long as I was with them, I guarded them in the pursuit of the life you gave through me; I even posted a night watch. And not one of them got away, except for the rebel bent on destruction. Now I'm returning to you. I'm saying these things in the world's hearing so my people can experience my joy completed in them. I gave them your word; the godless world hated them because of it, because they didn't join the world's ways, just as I didn't join the world's ways. I'm not asking that you take them out of the world but that you guard them from the Evil One. They are no more defined by the world than I am defined by the world. Make them holy—consecrated—with the truth; your word is consecrating truth. In the same way that you gave me a mission in the world, I give them a mission in the world. I'm consecrating myself for their sakes so they'll be truth-consecrated in their mission. I'm praying not only for them but also for those who will believe in me because of them and their witness about me. The goal is for all of them to become one heart and mind—just as you, Father, are in me and I in you, so they might be one heart and mind with us. Then the world might believe that you, in fact, sent me. The same glory you gave me, I gave them, so they'll be as unified and together as we are—I in them and you in me. Then they'll be mature in this oneness, and give the godless world evidence that you've sent me and loved them in the same way you've loved me. Father, I want those you gave me to be with me, right where I am, so they can see my glory, the splendor you gave me, having loved me long before there ever was a world. Righteous Father, the world has never known you, but I have known you, and these disciples know that you sent me on this mission. I have made your very being known to them—Who you are and what you do—And continue to make it known, so that your love for me might be in them exactly as I am in them.

I PRAY you are as thoroughly convinced as I am, after reading this prayer, that Jesus, the Son of God, wants you to be just like Him. He wants you to have the same depth of relationship with God that He has. It is almost incomprehensible that He desires us to have this depth of intimacy with God. I pray you will pursue this depth of intimacy with Him so when people see you, they will not be able to ascertain where He begins or ends in your life.

LUKE 23:34 – Jesus said, "Father, forgive them, for they do not know what they are doing." And they divided up his clothes by casting lots.

. . .

From Gethsemane to the cross, Jesus prayed. Right after being nailed to the cross, He prayed, "Father forgive them; for they know not what they do." While He was hanging there suffering from the beatings, and as the blood poured down His face, He prayed for the ones who had done this to Him. Jesus broke the silence not with wailing or anguish but with tender words filled with love, forgiveness, mercy, and compassion for those who were killing Him. In His agony, He interceded for them and also for us who would commit sin and stray from Him. These heartfelt words of forgiveness were the first words Jesus spoke directly from the cross to those who watched Him as He died. He not only prayed, but He forgave them all the atrocities they had done. Jesus asked His Father to forgive the ones who had hurt His Only-begotten Son. God forgave them as He also forgives us when we disobey and dishonor His Son.

Matthew 27:46 – At about three in the afternoon Jesus cried out in a loud voice, *"Eli, Eli lema sabachthani?"* that is, "My God, My God, why have You forsaken Me?"

Just before Jesus breathed His last breath, He cried out, "My God, My God, why have you forsaken Me?" As darkness covered the land Jesus felt alone and abandoned because He could no longer feel the presence of God. He had never experienced any degree of separation from His Father throughout His entire existence. It is evident from His cry that the aloneness was unbearable, so He spoke out His agony to God asking for His presence, and not to be forsaken. He is like us in this. Sometimes we feel abandoned by God and the ones we love the most but God did not forsake Jesus. In the moment that darkness covered the land, and the light of God's presence was removed, Jesus felt this profound loss. He felt the absence of God to such a degree that it was pure agony for Him. Keep in mind that in the eons of time Jesus had lived, He had never been separated from the Father, so this absence was deeply felt. But, as you know, God was always with His Son, He did not abandon Him. Three days later God raised Him from the dead and gave Him the place of highest honor. God has not abandoned you!

LUKE 23:46 – Jesus called out with a loud voice, "Father, into your hands I commit my spirit." When he had said this, he breathed his last.

RIGHT AFTER CRYING out to God, Jesus showed us He was aware God was with Him even to the very end. He prayed, "Father, into your hands I commit my spirit." He gave God the most important part of Himself, the part that has eternal value, His spirit. He relinquished His earthly tabernacle, the human flesh He had lived in for thirty-three years, and returned to what He had always been, a 'spirit being'. He was free from suffering and we will be free from suffering when we meet Him face-to-face.

LUKE 24: 30 – When he was at the table with them, he took bread, gave thanks, broke it, and began to give it to them.

AFTER HIS RESURRECTION, Jesus encountered some sad and distraught men on the road to Emmaus who were discussing His death. After encouraging and reminding them of the words Christ spoke about His suffering and resurrection, He prepared to leave them. They strongly urged Him to stay with them because it was late. As they sat at the table, He took bread, gave thanks, broke it, and gave it to them. Instantly their eyes were opened and they realized they were in the presence of the risen Christ. As soon as they recognized Him, Jesus disappeared from their midst. We too are challenged to hold on to the promises He has spoken over our lives when we are surrounded with trials and testing.

As the resurrected Christ, Jesus still prayed giving thanks to God for the food He was sharing with these men. When you and I bless our food, we are doing what He did. We are giving thanks to God for the provision because we recognize we would not have it without Him. We must remember that our jobs, and the salaries we receive from them, are not our source. It is God and only God who gives us provisions, therefore we should never miss an opportunity to say thank you.

LUKE 24:50 – When he had led them out to the vicinity of Bethany, he lifted up his hands and blessed them.

JUST BEFORE HIS ascension into heaven, Jesus led the disciples to the vicinity of Bethany, and there He lifted up His hands and blessed them. The final act Jesus performed was to pray for the disciples. He blessed them. May we be just like Him; willing, ready, and available at all times to pray for others. We should make it our priority to follow His example of always taking care of the needs of others.

One of the greatest gifts God has given us is the ability to connect with Him in prayer. We have direct access into God's presence when we invoke the name of Jesus. You and I have been given the opportunity to have an intimate relationship with the Father each time we pray. We get to share our heart concerns with Him and to hear His hopes and desires for us. We get to have an audience of one with the King of the Universe. This was made possible because Jesus said, "Yes," to the agony and suffering in the Garden of Gethsemane and on the cross.

The disciples asked Jesus to teach them how to pray and He did. We should also ask Him to teach us to pray so we can pray according to His will. In learning to pray as He does, we will get the right results each time we connect with Him. It is my heartfelt prayer that as you read this chapter, you gain wisdom and insight into the wonderful gift of prayer. Listen, if the Son of God prayed as often as He did, you and I have no option but to seek His face continually in prayer. Will you pray? We MUST pray!

Come with me as I share with you the prayer Jesus taught His disciples to pray in Matthew 6. Learning to pray the way Jesus taught them, will guarantee we connect with heaven each time we approach Him, and receive all our Father wants to give us.

LORD, TEACH ME TO PRAY

"Consider this, since you schedule many things, why not schedule the most important thing—time with God."

There are people who struggle with knowing how to pray, and what to pray for when they desire to commune with God. As a result of these uncertainties, some do not devote a great deal of time or concerted effort to prayer. There are also those who will reason, why pray at all because they have not received immediate responses to their prayers. Others may feel inadequate when praying so they do not seek after God consistently. People are at times intimidated when hearing others pray, and as a result, will not venture to pray in group settings. These trying situations and others have caused many people not to pursue God. At times it is hard to stay focused when praying because we may be conscious about some of these things. Also, because of a lack of consistency in prayer some have not yet discovered the joy, peace, hope, and contentment, they can experience each time they pray. Whatever has hindered your prayer walk, I encourage you to set it aside so you can come to know God in a more powerful and intimate way. This depth of intimacy can only be achieved through prayer.

I MUST pray, is a challenge to all of us. It reminds us prayer is not optional but must become central in our lives. As you read in the previous chapter, prayer was a MUST in the life of Jesus as He walked the earth. It was not optional to Him but was the main thing that kept Him on course while pursuing His destiny. Prayer kept Him steady and focused all the way to the cross.

After observing the consistent prayer life of Jesus and all He accomplished, the disciples realized that this was the key to success in their earthly assignments. They recognized that since prayer was essential to Jesus, it was also essential to them, so they asked Him to teach them to pray. There is no shame in admitting you need help in connecting to God in a more real, personal, and powerful way. You also have the same access to Jesus to ask Him to teach you how to pray. He will teach you so you can connect with the Godhead at any time and in all situations.

I want to devote this chapter to assisting you in developing a rich, full, and sustainable prayer life.

A close friend shared with me that over the years she had observed that many believers do not know how to pray effectively. As they pray, some do not feel they are praying correctly. When asked to pray, others will either pray the same rehearsed prayers or will pray something entirely different from what they were asked. I believe it is extremely important we pray as the Holy Spirit leads, and when we are asked to lead a specific prayer topic, it is important we pray what we are asked. If someone asks you to pray for sickness in their body, be sure to pray for God to heal them and not for the problems going on in the world.

Have you discovered that there are scriptures to cover every challenging situation you and others might be facing? When you know the Word, you can pray the Word. Praying the Word ensures you always know what to say to receive the right results. Praying the Word will also have an eternal and everlasting impact in the lives of people. Remember this—God did not leave us without the answers and the necessary tools to be successful in life. He has filled us with the Holy Spirit, who is our Teacher, for a reason. With the help of the Holy Spirit, we can attain what seems unattainable and have victory over everyday challenges. The challenge is we must get to know God's Word and spend time learning the ways and acts of the Holy Spirit. This equipping will ensure you are never uncomfortable when asked to pray, or when you see a need that requires God's intervention.

In the model prayer, Jesus taught the disciples some key elements that ensured effectiveness in their prayer life. As I highlight various prayer points, I pray you also find the answers you need to have both an effective and satisfying prayer life. Let's look at this prayer to glean what is needed to enrich our encounters with the Father.

He said to them, "This, then, is how you should pray: ""Our Father in heaven, hallowed be your name, your kingdom come, your will be done, on earth as it is in heaven. Give us today our daily bread. And forgive us our debts, as we also have forgiven our debtors. And lead us not into temptation, but deliver us from the evil one. Matthew 6:9-13 (NIV)

The first thing I want to point out is that the closing statement, "for thine is the kingdom and the power, and the glory, forever," is not a part of the original prayer. This closing is called a doxology and was added by Christians of the early Church who lived in the eastern half of the Roman Empire. In the Bible, we find this practice of concluding prayers with a short, hymn-like verse that exalts the glory of God. This was known as a climactic doxology with a passionate declaration of God's sovereignty.

In this model prayer are some key prayer points that will help us to obtain the things for which we are praying. We must have the right attitude when approaching God. Our hearts must be filled with thankfulness. We must worship Him telling of the amazing things He has done and all His wonderful attributes. Asking for forgiveness for ourselves and others must become an essential part of our prayer time. Remember to ask God to release you from temptations and to keep evil influences away from you.

In this model prayer, you will also find other key elements designed to strengthen your prayer life. Let's explore these eight things that will lead us to victory:

Knowing your position in God
A private place to meet with God
An attitude of praise/worship
God's presence and will revealed
God will provide for every need
God will pardon you
God will protect and deliver you
God is glorious and powerful

Knowing Your Position In God

I HAVE DISCOVERED in my journey with God that many of us do not fully understand who we are in Christ and the rights and privileges we have as God's sons and daughters. When we understand who we are in Him, we will have the courage and confidence to go to Him in prayer and believe Him for the answers. As Jesus taught the disciples to pray, He taught them God was their Father. A father is the source and the one who provides for the needs of his children. In Aramaic, the word 'Abba' is used to describe God, as Father. It signifies the close intimate relationship that our Father has with His children. God is Creator to all the people on the planet because He made them, but only born-again believers can rightfully call God, Abba. We alone can claim this depth of intimacy with Him because we have invited His Son into our hearts and given Him control of our lives. John 1:11-13 tells us this: He came to that which was his own, but his own did not receive him. Yet to all who did receive him, to those who believed in his name, he gave the right to become children of God—children born not of natural descent, nor of human decision or a husband's will, but born of God.

From this scripture, you see that when Jesus came, although God sent Him directly to His chosen people, the Israelites, most of them did not receive Him. As a result, those of us who were Gentiles were given the opportunity of knowing and claiming God as our Father. This gives us access to all He has for His children. Our God is a Life-Giver having all power and authority at His disposal. Because He is our Father, He disciplines us when we need correction. He instructs us in the way we should live. He guides and directs our lives. He corrects and rebukes us when we are wrong. He provides continual support to us, and He is actively involved with us. You can be assured of this—He always has your best interests at heart. I am encouraged to know God is intimately involved in our lives and wants access to every area to ensure that we succeed.

Let's consider the traits of a good earthly father. He is a provider and a protector, and he cares about the emotional and spiritual needs of his children. This means he will work even a menial job to ensure that there is food on the table. He will train and equip his children with biblical principles so they can succeed in life. This father will be sure to watch out for the emotional needs of his children. He will try his best to ensure they are not abused or harmed in any way, and that they are involved in healthy, godly relationships. Some of you can attest to this statement. Your parents would vet the person you were attempting to date before ever allowing them near you.

A good earthly father will train up his children based on biblical principles. Proverbs 22:6 tells parents to train up a child in the way they should go, and when they are old they will not depart from it. When time is invested in proper training, success will manifest. Parents who put forth effort to equip their children generally see that their efforts are invaluable. Most of these children usually make something of themselves and are not a burden on society. The promise in the scripture is if you train them correctly, even in old age they will cling to the training. Even if something happens later in life that causes them to drift away from their training, God promises they will eventually return. A godly father will lead by example, and stay involved with his children ensuring they remain steady in their love and devotion to God and family.

Now let's contrast our earthly Father with our heavenly Father. Jesus taught the disciples to acknowledge right at the onset who God is. He is the Father to those who have accepted Jesus as Savior and Lord. We each have the privilege of addressing God as 'Father'. This speaks volumes to me because it means we ALL have the same access to the blessings and provisions that only our heavenly Father can provide. Our Father loves His children equally. He is not partial to one over another. Unlike earthly parents who at times will have a partiality for one child over another, God loves all His children the same. Some children may appear to be more blessed than others, but I think this is a byproduct of the depth of their relationship with God and their level of obedience. In addressing God as our Father, Jesus points the disciples and us to our true source of help. Without God our lives are mediocre. We need God to infuse us with His love, wisdom, morals, and power. These virtues ensure we live victorious lives.

Jesus tells us that our Father resides in heaven. This clarifies for us that we are not looking to earthly fathers to bless us since they are limited in what they can do. God is the only One who has an unending supply of all we need. God's resources are limitless and we have access to Him, and all of them. When we accepted Jesus as Savior, God gave us the right to become joint heirs with His Son. The key point is that we have citizenship in heaven. The scriptures say we are born of God (1 John 5:1). This means God has intimate knowledge of us and wants us to have intimate knowledge of Him. When we truly comprehend this, we will never fail to run to God in prayer so He can meet our needs.

God has given us the highest position in Him. Ephesians 1 tells us God chose us before the creation of the world to be holy and blameless. It tells us He has blessed us in Christ with all spiritual blessings. He adopted us as His sons and daughters because it gave Him pleasure to do so. He has redeemed and forgiven us, lavishing us with wisdom and understanding. It tells us God has marked us with a seal. This seal is the promised Holy Spirit who is our deposit which guarantees our inheritance. This entire passage is a powerful reminder of who we are in Christ. I encourage you to take time to study the chapter so you can nail down your rights and privileges in God.

God has made us one in Christ Jesus. He has made us heirs and joint-heirs with His Son, which entitles us to all the rights and benefits of His Kingdom. This, then, is the reason we must grab hold of who we are in Him so we can truly connect with Him in prayer. When you know who you are, you act differently. You are not easily defeated, nor easily satisfied with mediocrity, always expecting better things for your life. You will have the confidence to know God has resources that are available to you, and be assured you have the backing of the Godhead so will never hesitate to go to God in prayer. You will find that your prayer time is not something to be endured but something to be enjoyed. As you pray, you get to have a one-on-one audience with the King of kings. Think about that! You get to enjoy God's presence without limitations. WOW!

Knowing your rights and position in God takes you beyond your limitations and helps you to truly know God as Abba, Father. Remember, you are welcomed at any time into God's presence, simply use the name of Jesus and watch as the resources of heaven become available to you.

A Private Place to Meet With God

LET me begin by saying you can pray anywhere and at any time because God is always listening and always hears you. That being said, having a private place where you can encounter God and connect to Him without constant distractions or interruptions is a must. Some people have a room in their homes that is devoted to prayer. Others may have a special spot where they meet with God. Still, others spend time in the outdoors under an open heaven. It does not matter where your specific place for encountering God is. What is important is that you set aside time daily to meet with Him face-to-face in the place you have designated.

I am aware some people spend time with God in the shower, or on the drive to work, but let me suggest something to you. Even though that is a good option, consider whether it is the best option. Why? It is vitally important we connect to God in prayer so we can receive wisdom, directions, and answers. Being able to sit still and hear Him is essential. Psalm 46:10 tells us to be *still* and know that He is God. In the stillness, you can hear Him more clearly. In the stillness, you can focus your heart and mind on Him. In the stillness, you will experience God more powerfully because nothing is distracting you from intimate fellowship. When we are distracted by other things, it is hard to hear clearly what God is speaking to our hearts. Consider this, since you schedule many things, why not schedule the most important thing—time with God? Make God a daily part of your schedule and this will ensure you have intimate encounters with Him regularly.

Throughout the years of developing my prayer life, I have met with God in different places. I have prayed in my closets, in different rooms throughout my home, outdoors, in my bedroom, during lunch hours at work, etc. The key was always to stop the busyness for a period of time and connect with God. In your private place, you will have a one-on-one audience with the God who hears and responds to your requests. You will never leave that place of intimacy without experiencing a greater connection with Him.

Jesus scheduled time away from His busyness to pray. He would find quiet places to commune with God. He often prayed on mountaintops, in the garden of Gethse-mane, in the wilderness, and in other lonely places (Matthew 14:23, Matthew 26:36, Luke 6:12, Luke 5:16). He seemed to have a preference for praying outside under an open heaven. What is important is you have a regular, consistent prayer life, and if designating a place to connect with God makes it easier to find your way to Him, then do it. Let's not miss a single opportunity to meet with Him.

An Attitude of Praise and Worship

WHY IS praise and worship so vital in our relationship with God? The simple answer is we were created for this very purpose. We are told in the scriptures that worship is ongoing in heaven. Saints and angels alike give continuous worship and praise to God. Think of His magnificence; of all the wonders He has created, including you, and you will find a multitude of reasons to praise Him. In the prayer in Matthew, Jesus taught us to focus on God, our Father. He instantly reminds us of what is most important—remembering who God is. With God as your focus, you are then able to communicate more intimately with Him.

Next, Jesus reminds us God's name is hallowed, His name is holy. The word hallowed means to be greatly revered, respected, and honored. As we enter times of prayer, we should first give God the worship He deserves. We must tell Him about His wonderful attributes and the great things He has done in our lives. Then must remind Him of who He is, and how He has blessed us, and give thanks for His continuous presence in our midst, especially during difficult seasons. You can often remind Him how greatly you appreciate His presence in your life. Our worship must be filled with thanksgiving because without God's protection, safety, help, and provisions, where would we be?

Throughout the scriptures, we find many instances of worship of our God. Everything in creation worships God. The birds sing their worship to Him, the waters roar their praises. Jesus said that if we do not give God the praise, the rocks will cry out in our place (Luke 19:40). From this we can infer that God will get His worship from whatever source is available and willing to give it. When you enter worship, come with the attitude that no matter what is going on in your life, or the world around you, you have decided to focus your heart and only give your allegiance to the King. When you decide to do this, understand the enemy will try his best to distract you in an attempt to take your focus off God. I have learned to turn down or turn off all phones when I need to connect to God. I make sure my cell phone is out of reach so I am not tempted to read the next text.

There are many distractions in the world, and the phone and internet are probably two of the greatest. Ask yourself this question, "When I am in a crisis do I want God's immediate, focused attention?" I am sure your answer is yes. Then consider that if you need His full, focused attention, why it is so incredibly hard to give Him yours. You will find such peace and comfort when you are lost in the presence of our King. When you are able to connect to Him, and clearly hear each word He is speaking to you, you receive comfort from the stresses of life. As you fix your heart to worship God, it is for no other reason than acknowledging He alone is God.

I do not worship God because He has answered all my prayers and my life is overflowing with blessings. As a matter of fact, I have worshipped God many times when exactly the opposite was happening. Worship is meaningful and powerful when we go to God in our distress and brokenness. Lifting your hands in surrender when your heart is breaking over various losses is a powerful act that tells God you trust Him in the face of difficulties. It is life-transforming to connect with Him while you are still waiting on answers. Though it might be extremely hard to give thanks and praise to anyone, including God, when you feel that your needs are unmet, worship takes you out of self. It is a selfless act. It says to God, "I am not sure why You have not yet moved on my behalf, but I am certain that when You are ready You will bring me justice." It also says, "I know You can change the outcome for me, even though You have not already done so, yet I will continue to give You what is already Yours—worship." This depth of trust does not come from believers who only seek God because of what they can get from Him, but from those who realize God is worshiped simply because He is God and He is good.

In my book, *Faith That Conquers*, I shared the story of my late friend, Mildred, who suffered from Lou Garrett's disease for many years. Throughout that ordeal, she continued to praise and worship God retaining that beautiful smile she always had. She did not allow the devil to steal either the joy or the smile from her face. One day I asked how she could continue to praise and give thanks when the possibility existed she would not recover without a miracle from God. Her response was simple but profound—I have decided to trust in the Lord regardless of what He chooses. I have previously shared that if she ever complained about her situation, only God heard it because none of us around her ever heard a word of complaint against God for allowing sickness to ravish her body. In contrasting her story with my own, I can say that in the past I have complained numerous times when I was sick even though my sickness was not unto death. I have complained when I was struggling with my finances, and I have also complained when relationships were not working out as planned. I know that some of you can attest to this. You have also complained instead of worshiping in the storms of life. You know what? You can change that today by choosing to worship God until He releases you from the struggles.

John 4:24 tells us that to worship God we must worship Him in spirit and in truth. We must give Him unending worship. To truly worship in spirit and in truth means we recognize that worship is not about us but all about God. Worship is adoration and devotion to the One we love. It is to glorify God in our service to Him and others. In our worship, we vow to honor God because He is God. We also worship because He has done amazing things for us. Consider these questions: Why do you worship God? What hinders your continual worship of Him? What is necessary to keep you worshiping even when faced with difficulties? Remember, power is released in greater measures when in brokenness you stand and lift your hands and voice, and say thanks to God who alone can change the outcome in your favor.

I encourage you not to let the rocks and other things that are not created in God's image to outdo you in worshiping Him.

God's Presence and Will Revealed

GOD DESIRES for each of us to know and understand the depth of His love for us. We have seen this throughout our lives. His presence is still with us even with all the wrong choices and mistakes we have made. He never distances Himself from us even when we are facing the consequences of our actions. In the midst of our pain, we can still hear the sweet whisper of the Holy Spirit as He comforts our wounded hearts. He wants you to know He longs to reveal His presence to you each time you pray no matter how devastated you may feel.

As you look at creation, you can see God's fingerprint in every facet of it. His presence is visible throughout the earth and we see evidence of it all around us. He is visible in the constantly changing sky. Each sunset and sunrise displays His beauty. We can hear His presence in the trees and winds that speak a language all of their own. God is even visible in the hills and mountains that are immovable. We find further evidence of His presence when we hear the tweeting of birds. Have you noticed that animals have languages only God understands? God is evident in creation because He created every living, breathing, thing that moves on the face of the earth. The birthing of a baby is evidence God exists. No one but God can birth a child into the earth. The healing of a sick body is evidence He is still very much involved in the affairs of mankind, and He is full of compassion for us. His intervention in our lives during seasons of crisis tells us His presence is a tangible thing if we will open our eyes and see His handiwork. God's will is evident to those who want to know His purposes for themselves. You will find His will as you read His Word. In every chapter of the Bible, God gives clear insight and direction to those who desire to know Him in a deeper way.

The coming of His Kingdom means we experience the presence of God in a profound way. Following are two people's definitions of the Kingdom of God: Anthony Hoekema describes God's Kingdom as "The reign of God dynamically active in human history through Jesus Christ, the purpose of which is the redemption of His people from sin and demonic powers, and the final establishment of the new heavens and the new earth." Graeme Goldsworthy's definition of the Kingdom of God is "God's people in God's place under God's rule."

Romans 14:17 tells us the Kingdom of God is not eating and drinking but righteousness, peace, and joy in the Holy Ghost. This tells me God wants His righteousness and peace to reign freely in our lives while we are on earth. He does not want us to simply benefit from this when we get to heaven. We especially need His joy and peace in the times in which we are living. As we pray, we get to ask Him to bring His Kingdom blessings into our lives right now. Luke 17:20-21 tells us the kingdom of God is within us.

What this says to me is that God's presence lives in the life of every believer in the person of the Holy Spirit. We have access to God's presence at all times by simply fellowshipping with the Holy Spirit. We can access His holiness, joy, peace, love, hope, strength, and all the other attributes that represent our God by asking Him daily to unfold His Kingdom promises in our midst. Make sure you also ask Him to make His will clearly known to you, so you will not miss a single thing He desires to birth in your life.

God Will Provide For Every Need

THE WORD IS FILLED with examples of God providing for the needs of His children; therefore, it is fitting that in the prayer Jesus taught the disciples to pray that it included praying for their daily bread. It is important to note the word 'daily'. It suggests God expects us to come to Him daily and petition Him for that day's needs. In our modern day and time, we seldom ask God for daily provisions because we buy what we need for weeks at a time. I think as a result of our abundance, we often forget that it is still God who provides. It is He who gives you the power to get the wealth (Deuteronomy 8:18). In asking God for our daily bread, we are constantly reminded He is the One who has provided the job, given us health to work it, and He is the only One who can sustain it.

From Genesis and through Jesus' time on earth, we read many stories of the Father's provision. Let's begin in Exodus to see His amazing provisions for His children.

THEN THE LORD said to Moses, "I will rain down bread from heaven for you. The people are to go out each day and gather enough for that day. In this way I will test them and see whether they will follow my instructions. On the sixth day they are to prepare what they bring in, and that is to be twice as much as they gather on the other days." Exodus 16:4-5 (NIV)

DID YOU SEE IT? God provided for their *daily* needs. Each day as they gathered the bread, they were not to gather more than they needed for that day or it would spoil. This means they could not horde the food. God used this as a test to see whether they would obey His instructions. God was making the point that in order to receive their daily provision they had to come to Him. Why was this so important? It was so they would not forget God and would learn to depend on Him for everything. God wanted continual communication and fellowship with them. He wanted them to be reminded He was their source of provision, their only source. If they neglected to remember this, they would think it was by their own ability and effort that they were sustained. I believe many people today, including some Christians, think it is by their own might that they are successful, but this is a deception of the devil.

Unfortunately, most Christians depend more on the companies they work for to meet their daily needs instead of God. We put more trust and confidence in our employers/companies than we do in God. It fascinates me that we can work for two weeks for a company, never seeing their bank account balances, but trust that after working the hours, they will have the resources to pay us. Yet, we struggle to hold on to the truth that God is the Source of all things. It has been God's intention from the beginning of creation to take care of the needs of His children, and He is still the One who provides for us today. Man was not created to bear the burden of his own provision, yet we have allowed ourselves to be ensnared by the world's ways of doing things rather than by God's. You have not attained what you have because of your efforts; rather it is by God's sustaining grace and power alone. If God did not awaken you each day, you would not have the material blessings you have.

God provided for the needs of the Israelites throughout their journey. He evicted others from the Promised Land to give His people access to the provisions, because He promised Abraham and his seed to bless them (Genesis 15:18. Following in the footsteps of His Father, Jesus also provided for the needs of the people. The scriptures tell me, that Jesus, after ministering to the crowds, would often feed them because He knew they were hungry. With a few loaves and fishes, He would ask God's blessing and feed thousands demonstrating His trust in God to multiply the meager supply to meet their needs. In blessing the small amounts of food among the people, He showed them that it was by the grace of God and His compassion that we are sustained.

Jesus demonstrated to the Israelites and to us that God was, and still is, our only Provider. Although many have turned away from Him and have begun depending on their own abilities, it is still by God's power that we have food, clothes, and shelter. Without His rain and sunshine, the crops would not produce a harvest, and we would not be able to sustain ourselves.

I can say conclusively that it is God who has provided for me and the needs in our ministries. From the day He launched the first ministry, He provided. When He gave me the instructions to begin developing the ministry, He also gave me the finances to get all the materials printed. This is how He provided. After finalizing the preparatory work, I did not have the funds to print the brochures and cards needed to promote the ministry. One Sunday morning while serving at church, a single mom who had three children came looking for me. She had limited resources but God used her anyway. She gave me a card and said the Lord emphatically told her not to leave the church without giving it to me. I thanked her and later when I opened the card it contained the exact amount I needed to print the materials to launch the ministry.

Throughout the last ten years, I have witnessed God's faithfulness in providing for our needs. At times the journey has been long and arduous but I am always reminded He promised to supply my daily needs. From our first mission trip to Honduras to today, He has amply provided not only for me and the team but also for the thousands we have clothed and fed. With all the local and international mission outreaches to the poor, widows, and orphans we have conducted over the last ten years, time and again, He has proven to be faithful. As a result of this, our faith in God has increased significantly from year to year.

Six months after launching the ministry, I went on my first ministry trip to Honduras. God began the work of testing my obedience and my faith in what He could accomplish. We served in a very poor community and I met a pastor who was doing all she could to meet the needs of the poor children. She had an old beat-up station wagon that barely functioned as a usable vehicle, and would load as many children as possible into it, then did her best to get them to where they needed to be. After witnessing this a few times, one morning in prayer I heard God say to get her a van. Let's remember, I had just launched the ministry six months earlier and did not have the funds to even print the materials.

I was only on the mission trip because someone had paid the fare and the hotel so I could go and minister, yet God asked me to buy this lady a van. My response was dismissive, "This definitely is not God speaking to me," so I proceeded with my prayer and heard the same words again. This time I responded by asking Him this, "Where in the world could I possibly get the money to buy her a van?" His simple but straightforward answer to me was to trust Him. After my initial doubt that God had spoken to me about getting this van, I surrendered to Him.

Later in the week, I held a conference and Pastor Martha was there. The Lord instructed me to take her to dinner to get to know her better and to hear about the vision she had for the children. God works in surprising ways when He wants to get His message across. Our driver forgot to pick us up after the conference so the only way to get to dinner was to ride in the Pastor's car. When I told my team member we would ride with her, the horror on her face was priceless. I still laugh out loud every time I think of it. The car was even worse than I realized. It struggled to reach the proper speed and the people around us were constantly blowing their horns at her. After that harrowing experience, I was convinced I heard God and began to pray for His provisions as I prepared to return to the USA. My team member informed me I should have said yes to God sooner, so He did not have to prove to me He had indeed spoken to me. Upon arriving in the USA, I began to share with various people the charge God had given me to buy the pastor a van, and God faithfully provided it. I will share the remainder of the story in an upcoming chapter.

Whatever you need from God, remember He is the same yesterday, today, and forever (Hebrews 13:8). When you pray His Word and remind Him of His promises, He is faithful to answer and provide. He will provide all your needs according to His riches in glory in Christ Jesus.

God Will Pardon You

ONE OF THE greatest gifts we, as believers, enjoy is forgiveness. Jesus' sacrifice on the cross was to provide salvation, included in which is forgiveness of sin. We have the privilege of being able to go to the Father when we have fallen short of His standards to ask His pardon and forgiveness. The word pardon means—forgiveness, absolution, clemency, mercy, leniency, and remission. 1 John 1:9 says that if we confess our sins He is faithful and just to forgive us and to cleanse us from all unrighteousness. It is important to note that the promise in the scripture is conditional. You must do something in order to be cleansed and forgiven. You must confess your sins and must tell God what you have done. It is not enough to go to God with generalities, we must be specific in telling Him what sins we have committed and then ask Him to release and pardon us. I find it interesting that many people today hesitate to call sin, sin. We use terms such as these—I messed up, I fell short, that was not God's best for me, I made a mistake, and this list is ongoing but you get the picture. We try to make sin more tolerable by not really stating that we have sinned against God. Remember, it is God we have sinned against not ourselves or even against man. God is asking us to admit our wrongdoing so He can release us from the burden of guilt and shame.

Have you discovered yet that sin causes you to feel shame and guilt? At times sin will cause you to feel worthless, and these feelings can contribute to other negative behaviors. We experience these negative behaviors because we are attempting to cover up the wrongs we have committed, and also the feelings of guilt that are associated with them. The enemy is determined to keep us in this negative cycle because it keeps us pursuing the wrong things. Jesus offers us freedom from guilt and shame by His death on the cross.

Over the years, I have heard many powerful stories of people forgiving others. I have come to realize, however, that it is not only important God and others forgive us, but we must also forgive ourselves for the wrongs we have committed. Until we forgive ourselves, we will struggle to fully receive the forgiveness Jesus died to give us. The challenge is that although He has forgiven us, we allow the devil to play the broken 'sin' records of how badly we have messed up over and over in our minds. As we attempt to move forward and do something significant with our lives, the enemy whispers his lies into our ears. He reminds us of the secret sins we have committed and then asks what makes us qualified to do anything of value. What he does is he shames us into silence. He causes us to question our integrity, morality, and worthiness. We need to remember, however, that we are not worthy because of anything we have done, we are only worthy because of what He did, Jesus made us worthy.

For many years I would go to God in prayer and ask forgiveness for the same sins over and over again. One day, I was yet again asking God for His forgiveness when He said, "Joan, what are you talking about? I forgave you years ago when you confessed and I do not remember the sin anymore. The problem you face is not that I have not forgiven you, but it is you have not forgiven yourself. When I say I do not remember, I mean I do not remember because I have chosen to keep no records of your offenses since you have repented and turned away from them. Forgive yourself and move forward." His response to me in this instance was very firm because I continuously presented the same matter before Him. I had not yet real-ized I had the power to set myself free from the enemy's condemnation. I simply needed to admit to God that I had sinned, genuinely repent, forgive myself, turn away from the sin, and then cancel all accusations of the devil with the Word of God. I took my power back by casting down every lie the devil attempted to whisper in my ears.

The devil's goal is to stop you from ever feeling good

enough about yourself to break the negative cycle and accomplish something of value with your life. Jesus came to pardon and forgive you. He wants you free so you can live life to its fullest; and when you are free, you will more readily embrace the assignments He has for you. Remember, forgiveness is not just to free the offender, no, the greatest reason we forgive is to secure our own freedom. Should we choose to not exercise forgiveness, we lock ourselves in the prison of our minds. We also have a tendency to rehearse the offenses and this causes us to become angrier, which is exactly what the enemy wants. Consider that often the person who offended you may not even be aware of it or may have simply forgotten they have offended you. At other times they may not care about the hurt they have inflicted on you; they have moved on yet you still carry the scars from the wounds. Forgiveness frees you from the wounds of the past. Forgiveness is first and foremost for you.

I am so grateful that our loving Father, God, has chosen to release us from the bondage of sin and shame through the power of His forgiveness. There are numerous scriptures that speak about forgiveness, forgiving, and pardon. It is important to God we forgive so we can receive His forgiveness. Matthew 6:15 says that if we do not forgive men their trespasses then our Father will not forgive us. I can say unequivocally that I need God's forgiveness on a daily basis, so I strive to be quick about forgiving others even though at times it is not an easy task. Remember, the scripture says that as far as the East is from the West, so far has He removed our sins and transgressions from us (Psalm 103:12). Therefore, in order for us to experience this total forgiveness let's quickly forgive others.

God Will Protect and Deliver You

CAN you think of a time in your life when you knew without a shadow of a doubt that God protected you? One of the promises in the prayer He taught the disciples was that His protection and deliverance are available to us. Some of you can instantly remember a time when He protected you while others may have to give it some thought. I guarantee you that at some time in your life you have experienced the protection and deliverance of the Lord. I vividly remember how He saved my life a few years ago. I was coming from a meeting and heading to Atlanta to catch a flight to Houston when I was involved in an accident. I had my praise and worship songs playing and was singing to the Lord when an eighteen-wheeler drifted into my lane and hit me causing my rental car to spin out of control. So you can get the full impact of the story, I need to back up and tell you how unbeknownst to me God prepared me for this accident. The meeting had turned into a nightmare for me, so for the entire trip God gave me Psalm 34 to read and meditate on. Let's read the scripture together to see what it says:

I WILL EXTOL the LORD at all times; his praise will always be on my lips. My soul will boast in the LORD; let the afflicted hear and rejoice. Glorify the LORD with me; let us exalt his name together. I sought the LORD, and he answered me; he delivered me from all my fears. Those who look to him are radiant; their faces are never covered with shame. This poor man called, and the LORD heard him; he saved him out of all his troubles. The angel of the LORD encamps around those who fear him, and he delivers them. Taste and see that the LORD is good; blessed is the man who takes refuge in him. Fear the LORD, you his saints, for those who fear him lack nothing. The lions may grow weak and hungry, but those who seek the LORD lack no good thing. Come, my children, listen to me; I will teach you the fear of the LORD. Whoever of you loves life and desires to see many days, keep your tongue from evil and your lips from speaking lies. Turn from evil and do good; seek peace and pursue it. The eyes of the LORD are on the righteous and his ears are attentive to their cry; the face of the LORD is against those who do evil, to cut off the memory of them from the earth. The righteous cry out, and the LORD hears them; he delivers them from all their troubles. The LORD is close to the brokenhearted and saves those who are crushed in spirit. A righteous man may have many troubles but the LORD delivers him from them all; he protects all his bones, not one of them will be broken. Evil will slay the wicked; the foes of the righteous will be condemned. The LORD redeems his servants; no one will be condemned who takes refuge in him.

Psalm 34:1-22 (NIV)

As I STATED EARLIER, the trip was not going well so the Lord told me to read this passage each day and night. It helped me to remain calm and peaceful so I would not speak or do anything out of anger, which would have given me a poor testimony. Now, in retrospect, as I read this passage I see that because I listened to the Word and kept my heart pure and my tongue from evil, God stepped in and saved my life. As the meeting progressed, I realized I was not in agreement with the leader and did not like many of the things I was now learning about her. Unfortunately, the situation escalated to unpleasant levels, so I moved to another hotel and rented a car to drive back to Atlanta by myself. When the rental arrived it was extremely small, I called it a toy car. When we arrived at the rental office, I felt a strong prompting from the Holy Spirit to ask the agent for a larger car. He was very firm with me about getting a larger car even though the cost was higher. I am so grateful I heard and obeyed His instructions or I might not be here today.

When the eighteen-wheeler hit me it was going about eighty miles per hour. It was so sudden. One moment I was singing praises to God and the next moment the car was spinning out of control. As I was zigzagging across the freeway I realized the driver's side of my car was attached to the eighteen-wheeler. I only had time to say, "JESUS". Eventually, the car, with me in it, ended up several lanes over and in a ditch. When it stopped, it was still attached to the bumper of the eighteen-wheeler. I scrambled to safety out the passenger door. A couple pulled over to check on me. The first words out of the man's mouth were, "Lady, who are you?" He told me that as they watched the accident he said to the Lord several times, she is not going to make it. Each time it appeared the car was going to roll over it was as if someone pushed it upright, and it would land right side up again. He said, "I don't know who you are, but I know God has a great plan for your life to save you as He did today." His wife was a Paramedic and she checked me out to see that I was okay before they left. They were on their way to Atlanta to pick up their daughter who was returning from a mission trip. How like God to send Christians to help me in my time of need.

As I write this testimony, I am once again reminded of how greatly loved we are and how God protects His children. From telling me to study the promises in Psalm 34; to insisting I get a larger vehicle; to having His angels encamped about me; and keeping the car from rolling over; He was there every step of the way. Once the driver of the eighteen-wheeler got over his horror, he came to check on me and relayed the reason he kept the truck attached to the car was that 'something' told him if he released it I would roll over and not survive, so he obeyed the voice he heard. The Holy Spirit spoke to this man who was not a believer and told him what to do to save my life, but the story does not end there.

The accident took place in an area of the freeway where there were no gas stations, no businesses, and no hotels for miles. The police officer who assisted me called a wrecker to get the car. When he discovered the rental company had no offices within two hours of where I was, he took me several miles down the road to a car dealership. I later discovered the people were his friends and he knew they would help me get to Atlanta. They were most helpful and found a couple to drive me to Atlanta later that evening. Once again God sent believers to take care of me until I was safely in the hotel in Atlanta. One final thing God did that is a reminder of His protection and love, is that in the midst of this chaos, my Pastor, Tim Barker, in Houston felt impressed by the Lord to pray earnestly for me. After he finished, he called to see if I was okay. I had just arrived at the dealership and shared with him what had happened. He prayed with me and comforted me in the midst of the crisis. God is so personal with His children. He is not some distant Father who is not concerned. If I had ever wondered whether He was faithful to His Word—to protect and deliver us, He demonstrated He is always faithful.

When I arrived safely at the hotel, I bowed my knees to express my thanks for His protection, His angels surrounding me, and all the people He sent along the way to help me. He prompted me to pick up my Bible and reread Psalm 34. As I read through the verses again, He highlighted a section I had not seen clearly until that moment. Verses 19-20 say, "A righteous man may have many troubles, but the LORD delivers him from them all; *he protects all his bones, not one of them will be broken.*" Not one of my bones was broken, praise the name of the Lord! Finally, not only did God have me to study Psalm 34, but He led one of my faithful team members, Gloria, to the same passage and had her pray it daily over me while I was away.

God protects and delivers His children. He keeps us from being annihilated by the enemy. Not only is the Lord's Prayer filled with promises of protection and deliverance, but so are many other scriptures in the Bible. I encourage you to search through its pages and let God lead you to His promises for your life. I encourage you to take these promises from Psalm 34 and ask God to cause them to become alive in you.

Promises for Protection (Psalm 34)

When you seek God, He will hear you.

He will deliver you from all your fears.

He will never allow you to be covered with shame.

When the poor call, God hears them and saves them from all their troubles.

The angel of the Lord encamps around those who fear God.

God will instruct His angels to deliver you.

You can take refuge in God.

When you fear God and stand in awe of who He is, you will lack nothing.

When you stay away from evil and speak the truth, you will enjoy life and have many good days.

The eyes of the Lord are on the righteous, YOU!

God is attentive to your cries for help.

God delivers the righteous from all their troubles.

The Lord is close to the brokenhearted.

He saves those who are crushed in spirit.

God protects the righteous; not one of their bones will be broken.

The Lord redeems His children, and will not condemn us when we take refuge in Him.

I pray you meditate on these promises and engrave them in your heart. I also pray that like me, when you need them, they will manifest in your life and bring you hope, help, deliverance, and protection.

God is Glorious and Powerful

I CANNOT CONCLUDE this chapter without sharing how glorious and powerful God is. The mere fact He would teach the disciples and us this amazing prayer lets us know He is for us. As we look in-depth into the prayer He taught the disciples, it is important to note that praising God is a significant component of this prayer. The prayer begins with praises to God. It acknowledges who God is and where He resides. He not only resides in heaven but more importantly, He resides in us. Therefore, it is fitting that Jesus would conclude the prayer with a reminder of who God is and what He does. We are reminded that He is the only Kingdom worth mentioning. All other kings and kingdoms pale in comparison to His. No other king created the universe and all that is in it, but God. No other king controls the days and seasons, but God. No other king breathed his breath of life into man and continues to sustain us, but God. No other king has the power to govern us and the universe, but God. No other king has redeemed man from destruction, but God, and no other king will come again to take us to the home He has prepared for us, but God. I think you get the picture! He is all glorious and all-powerful.

To say God is glorious means He is to be celebrated. His fame is world renown and we see His glory throughout the entire universe. God is to be acclaimed and honored at all times. He is wonderful, marvelous, and magnificent. All the works of His hands are perfect. He does extraordinary things not only in the affairs of men but in all facets of the universe. Our God's glory outshines all others. His remarkable acts are a wonder to behold. As brilliant as the stars in the skies are, they are only a dim reflection of the brilliance of our Creator. When we think of how glorious God is, we cannot help but think of a beauty and splendor that evokes feelings of wonder, excitement, and total admiration for Him. God has done spectacular things in us and all around us, so when we pray we must remember to whom we are praying and give Him the honor, respect, and reverence He deserves.

God is all-powerful. He has the ability to influence mankind and everything in the created world. His influence is far-reaching and His authority is limitless. Our God is a God of great power who compels mankind to act in accordance with His will. The wonders He has created compel us to acknowledge that there is a greater force at work in the universe and that things do not occur randomly or by happenstance. He is strong and mighty and He is a force to be reckoned with. As we consider who God is, remember, that He is our Father.

As the early Christians concluded the prayer with this doxology, "For Thine is the kingdom, and the power and the glory, forever and ever, amen," know to whom you are pledging your allegiance. Every time you pray, this glorious, powerful, and amazing Being is completely in tune with you. You will always have an audience of one with Him at any time you choose to connect with Him in prayer. I pray you will use the great tools Jesus gave us in this prayer to deepen your prayer life. When you do, may you experience an increase of His power and anointing in your life, and behold all the wonders He will perform as you make time to seek His face regularly.

WHY ARE MY PRAYERS UNANSWERED

"If the last sin you committed caused you to feel that there is no point in praying because you have messed up so badly, then the enemy is winning."

The question of unanswered prayers plagues us all. Many of us can concur that there are several prayers we have prayed, for which we have not yet received answers. We are not entirely sure why these prayers are unanswered, and at times, can feel despondent or even discouraged. In addition, we can truthfully say we do not know the formula for getting God to move on our behalf. To some, it appears they are not even close to getting the breakthroughs even after the many hours spent seeking His face. It is my goal in this chapter to help you see when the delays are either by God's design, because of our choices, or because of the enemy. There are times when God is not ready to manifest the answers so He delays us. At other times we are delayed as a result of either our wrong expectations or because the enemy delays us.

Whatever the reason for the delays, we can be assured of this, God always answers prayers. Sometimes the answer is yes, no, or wait. We must know which one of the three is God's answer for us so we can position ourselves to receive.

Before we dive into the reasons why prayers may not be answered, let's first listen to this story of a prayer that was answered because it will give us a few insights into why we don't always receive our answers. As you read, you will see instances where this prayer could have gone unanswered because of my disobedience, doubt, and unbelief.

As I shared in chapter three, on my very first mission trip, God gave me what I felt was an impossible assignment. After meeting Pastor Martha who was taking care of children in a poor community, it was apparent she needed transportation to help her get around and take care of the children. The day God spoke to me about getting her a van, was the day after I saw her load ten-plus children into her little car. The next morning in prayer, God clearly told me to buy her a van but I did not respond with absolute obedience. Remember, I had just started the ministry and had no finances, therefore you will understand my reaction. I acted as if I had not heard God. When He spoke the words again I responded with, "That is not God, He knows I have no money." So for the next few days, I continued to hear the same words but was still not accepting what I heard. God has this amazing way of getting His point across.

As I shared earlier, I had to ride in her car. Wow, what an experience that was. Her car was old; the inside of the ceiling was torn and raggedy, the seats were worn out, and it struggled to get enough power to keep moving. Other drivers all around us were blowing their horns at her because the car struggled to move from one intersection to another. I knew then God was making it abundantly clear He had spoken to me, and He drove the message home by allowing me to ride in her car. I repented for not saying yes and responding to His instructions quicker and then asked for wisdom as to how to proceed with raising the funds for the van.

When I returned to the USA I shared this with several people, and within a few months, God provided the money to buy the van. God also provided the money to ship the van to Honduras. Six months later, when the van was presented to Pastor Martha, we discovered how truly faithful God was and how He works. For years she had been praying for God to give her an SUV, and no one believed God would do it, including her husband. When she saw the vehicle, tears began to fall, and we discovered her favorite color was blue and that was the color she asked God for. Listen, God heard her prayer, and years later answered it precisely.

I shared this story with you to make a point. Sometimes our prayers are unanswered because at times we do not obey the instructions of the Holy Spirit and miss opportunities. As a result of my struggles with finances, I did not believe God was speaking to me about getting her the van. I doubted I heard God because I could not see how this was possible since I was living in such lack, and I did not understand that when God gives the vision He always gives the provision.

In this chapter, I want us to look at a few reasons I believe that our prayers are unanswered. There are many others, but I want to focus on these three because I believe they are some of the top reasons we experience delays or why we feel our prayers have gone unanswered.

Disobedience Delays Our Answers

OBEDIENCE IS one of the greatest keys to God releasing His blessings into our lives. When we are quick to obey, God is pleased and will do miracles in our midst. A lack of obedience has caused many of us to miss out on some amazing miracles, blessings, and opportunities. When God speaks we must be quick to say, "Here I am Lord, use me." Because we do not respond in the right way or in obedience, the answers to our prayers are often delayed.

Disobedience has been a stumbling block in the path of great men and women for centuries. It began in the Garden of Eden and we are still suffering the consequences today. In Genesis 2 when Adam and Eve listened to the devil and disobeyed God, they reaped the consequence of their disobedience and were expelled from paradise. Later their older son, Cain, killed his younger brother, Abel, and they had to start again when God gave them a third son, Seth. From that first act of disobedience until today, mankind has been plagued with struggles. We often expect God to overlook our acts of disobedience and bless us anyway but that is not how God works. God is a God of order and obedience is one of the laws He established in the earth.

1 Samuel 15:22 says that obedience is better than sacri-

fice. This tells us God prefers us to say yes to His will rather than bringing Him a sacrificial offering because of disobedience. I know at times it seems more convenient to take the easy way out, for example, it may appear less complicated to tell a lie than admit to the truth. We think that in telling a lie we are getting away with it, but truth always wins over lies. The scripture tells us that whatever is hidden will be exposed (Luke 8:17). How many of you can attest to the truth that in your life, and in the lives of many people you have known, sooner or later any wrong-doings always surface? This is played out in our churches, in corporate America, in relationships, and families around the world. What is hidden will not stay hidden for long it will eventually be exposed to the light.

Think about it this way, when you add cream to coffee that cream eventually rises to the surface, it does not stay hidden in the bottom of the cup. This shows us that whatever is done in darkness will eventually surface as well because that is simply how life works. When this happens and we are exposed, God is there to help us pick up the pieces. He allows exposure because He is after something greater than our reputations, He is after our character. God is intent on conforming the believer into the image of His Son, Jesus Christ. When we choose obedience over disobedience, however, God will walk with us through the difficult seasons ahead.

Disobedience causes delays because it essentially ties the hands of God and prevents Him from moving on our behalf. From Adam until now, God has been looking for people who will simply obey Him. He found that person in His Son, Jesus, but unfortunately from the time of Jesus until now many have continued to be just plain disobedient. Now, I am not saying that there are not people who strive with all their hearts to obey God, but at times we miss the mark. For each person trying to obey the voice of God, there are, unfortunately, probably many more ignoring Him and His instructions. Since we are only responsible for governing ourselves let's make sure we are quick to obey so God can be glorified through us.

Disobedience can take many different forms. At times we will say no to doing what is right. We can develop an uncaring attitude to the plights of others even though God tells us to take care of the needs of the less fortunate, and then justify our inaction to make our decision seem more palatable. We sometimes also pretend not to hear or understand what is being asked of us. Some choose to do it their way because they think their way is the best way. Whatever the reasons for the disobedience, the consequences will be the same—you will not have the support and protection of the God-Head. When the answers to your prayers are delayed and you ask yourself, why, consider your last act of disobedience. What was the last thing God told you to do that you didn't do? When you realize how you did not comply with His request, go back and rectify the situation so God can answer you. I think the question is worth asking, "If I disobeyed the last instruction God gave me, will I receive the thing which I am requesting?" I believe as you contemplate this question, and answer it honestly, you will find the answer to why so many prayer requests go unanswered. I have learned that when I have waited an exceedingly long time for God to answer me, I need to go back and check to see what the last thing He told me to do, and see if I obeyed. When I discover that I have not obeyed, I quickly repent and proceed to act in obedience to His will. Love for God equals obedience and obedience will get you a breakthrough in your prayer life every time.

A Lack of Faith

SOME OF US can admit we have a hard time believing God will act on our behalf. It is especially difficult if we have waited an inordinate length of time and have seen no tangible results. Is it possible that the longer the delay, our faith and confidence in God's ability to perform begins to erode? Why is it so hard to nail down our faith in God? Let me suggest a few things and I invite you to add to this list:

- We have not received answers to some of our deepest prayer requests
- We have prayed for people and the outcomes were unfavorable. (They were diagnosed with the disease and died; they lost their spouse through divorce; or lost their jobs, etc.)
- We are still struggling in our own life—health, home, and finances
- We have not experienced the abundant favor that others are enjoying
- We feel as if God has abandoned us
- We feel God is unwilling to help us even though in our estimation, we have given our all to Him

Whatever your reason for not having absolute faith in God, let's try to rectify this now. Yes, you have prayed and yes, a number of those prayers are yet to be answered. This does not mean God did not hear you and He will not answer you. It simply means He is either not ready to give the answers or, He has something better in store for you which requires a longer season of waiting. I know this place well! I could give you a long list of things I am also waiting for God to respond to, and have to hold tightly to my faith believing He has heard me and will answer.

At times the journey of faith is extremely difficult because you cannot assess why you are not connecting to God, and why you are delayed. Is He saying no, yes, or wait? If you are asking in accordance with His will and His Word, then you can be assured He will respond. If, however, you know that what you are praying for does not line up with His will for you, then you already know the answer to your request is no, so release it and move forward trusting He knows what is best for you.

Hebrews 11:1 says that faith is being sure of what we hope for and certain of what we do not see. As you continue reading this chapter, you find that from the very beginning men and women had to operate in faith so God could move on their behalf. This passage records the stories of many of God's generals of faith. Some of these died having never received the answers to their prayers this side of heaven, but it tells us they were still living by faith when they died. The scriptures say they did not receive the things promised; they only saw them and welcomed them from a distance. What this tells me is that even though they did not get a hold of their promises, the generations that followed received the things for which they prayed. Don't ever stop praying!

In this chapter alone the charge to live by faith is strong. We find the statement, 'by faith', recorded twenty-one times. By faith, these generals of God continued to hope and trust in Him until the very end. They did not give up on their requests because they considered that God was faithful to keep His promise. You and I must pray that God will increase our faith. Let's ask Him to increase it to such a degree that we will never give up on Him no matter how long we wait. I have decided that I not only *believe* that God can do it, I *know* He can. I have moved from simply believing to absolutely knowing God can and will answer me. How about you?

From the list above we see that we often lose faith because we have not received our requests. Because many of these requests are near and dear to our hearts, we are a bit confounded that they appear not to be of top priority to God. We think because He has not yet moved He has ignored our requests, but that is not true. God does not consider even our simplest request to be insignificant. Every prayer is heard, and every tear is seen and given His attention.

Psalm 56:8 is one of my favorite scriptures because it tells us how important we are to God. It says, "You keep track of all my sorrows.

You have collected all my tears in your bottle. You have recorded each one in your book." God sees and records our tears. He is such a loving and good Father that even our tears are important to Him. I have anchored my hope in this—since my tears are so important He records them, I am convinced He will answer me at the right time and give me victory. Let this become your hope as well.

After you have prayed, whether for yourself or for someone you love, you must leave the answer in the capable hands of the Savior. He is aware that the diagnosis will come, that people will divorce, that others will lose their jobs, and that some of the people you are praying for will die, but He is still with you in every crisis. As you read that statement some of you may be thinking, "But why?" That is the mystery. This is where faith in Him must become paramount in our lives. We must simply trust there are greater things at work in our situations that we cannot yet see or comprehend.

Deuteronomy 29:29 tells us that the secret things belong to the Lord our God, but the things revealed belong to us and to our children forever. We must trust His wisdom. Understand this, "Every struggle will birth something great in the life of the person enduring the struggle."

I have counseled many people who were either diagnosed with a disease, going through a divorce or lost a job, who struggled to stay afloat. In many cases, some recognized they were stronger than they ever thought they were. Through their crises, they discovered they could face any difficulties and still overcome them. I have a close friend who went through a divorce. I asked her what she discovered through the painful ordeal and her response was, "I am stronger than I thought I was." She discovered God was always with her and she could trust Him to see her through. Her faith in God grew as a result of this difficult situation. This is one of the mysteries. The things sent by the enemy to destroy you are used by God to strengthen and draw you closer to Him, and to increase your faith.

As you position yourself and solidify your trust and faith in God, let me remind you of a few things. God is with you in the struggles. He does not love others more than He loves you. He has abundant favor in store for you. He will never abandon you. When you serve Him, giving Him all you have, He does not discount it and is pleased by your devotion. He is pleased that you have made Him the center of your life.

I was reminded by a friend how God favors His children. Each day this friend prays Luke 2:52 over himself and his family. It says, "Jesus grew in wisdom and stature and in favor with God and man." Since praying this, he gets continual favor wherever he goes. I also began declaring this scripture over myself and have personalized it to get the maximum results in my life. I declare daily that Joan grows in wisdom and stature and in favor with God and man. I hope you will make this scripture part of your daily declarations as well then watch to see God's power and favor unfold in your life. The key is to gain favor with God first, and then He will give you favor with men, women, and children.

Remember, you gain everything when you anchor your faith, hope, and trust in the Lord our God.

A Lack of Persistence

HAVE you ever pursued something you thought you really wanted, and then ran out of steam before you received it? At the inception, you prayed consistently and stood in great faith, but the longer you waited the less persistent you became. Your lack of persistence was not because you did not still desire the thing you initially pursued, but the work that was necessary to attain it became burdensome, and you did not want to continue to put forth the effort. Some of our prayer life is like this example. We begin with great fervor, excitement, and determination, but the longer we pray without seeing results we lose our fire and passion for prayer.

To persist means we must do what 1 Thessalonians 5:17 tells us, "To pray without ceasing." This does not mean the only thing you do is to pray all day and neglect your responsibilities, it means you can have an attitude of prayer throughout the day. When you have breaks in your day, you can utter a prayer or give thanks to the Lord. Years ago, I was at a conference with a few friends and one of them asked me this question, "Do you know that you are always singing?" I did not realize this until she asked the question. Whenever I am not busy, I am always humming or singing a song. At the time she asked the question I had no idea how long I had been doing this, but it is now twenty-five years later, and I still hum or sing to the Lord throughout the day. This is my act of keeping Him close by.

Persistence is the quality in you that allows you to continue doing or trying something even in the face of opposition. It often means going beyond the usual way of operating and doing something outside the norm. Some of you will persist until you get the results you are after. You refuse to accept the option to quit. The Bible is filled with scriptures and stories of persistence, and I will share a few of those so you get a clear understanding that it is those who persist, who keep asking, and who keep going to God, who are the ones that will receive the prize.

Galatians 6:9 says to let us not become weary in doing good, for at the proper time we will reap a harvest if we do not give up. It is clear then you will get weary in the pursuit and feel like quitting, but if you quit then you negate the results you are after. Now apply that to your prayer life. What are you praying for? How important is the answer to this request? If it has real value to you, then you will persist in prayer until you get the answer you seek. The scripture has a promise for those who refuse to quit. You will reap a harvest. What harvest? The answer to your prayers! A breakthrough in the situations of your life. The right door will open for you at the proper time. This proper time is God's perfect timing for your life and the unfolding of His blessings in your midst. Don't give up on your prayer time with God.

Luke 11:9-10 tells you to ask and it will be given to you; seek and you will find; knock and the door will be opened to you. For everyone who asks receives: the one who seeks finds; and to the one who knocks, the door will be opened. Let's unpack the promises in these verses. God has given us the secret in these two verses for obtaining the blessings—

PERSISTENCE. To receive, you must ask in prayer for what you want. You have to keep asking until you receive. To get the right doors to open in your life, you must approach the door and knock until someone opens it to you. God is the One who opens doors for you to receive the blessings when you pray; therefore, if you do not approach Him you will not gain entrance into His blessings.

The promises in the scripture are clear and they are also conditional. You <u>must</u> do something to get what you want. Everyone who <u>asks</u> receives—if you have not yet received keep asking until you do. The one who <u>seeks</u> finds —if you have not yet found the answers then keep seeking until you do. To the one who <u>knocks</u> the door will be opened—if the door has not yet opened for you then go back and keep knocking until it does. The scripture did not say only a few people will receive, it says EVERYONE and that includes you. So if you have prayed long and hard, and the answers have not yet arrived, keep praying until they do because God cannot lie, and His Word cannot fail. His Word will produce a harvest in the life of anyone who believes and applies it.

Proverbs 24:16 tells us that although the righteous fall seven times, they rise again. Along the journey, you will stumble and fall at times, but the key is you don't stay down, you must rise up. No matter how difficult, embarrassing, and painful it might be to stand and face the issues, you must get back up and get back in the race. Often we are knocked down because the enemy wants to keep us from moving closer to God and our assignments; at other times we are knocked down because of unwise choices. We may have done things we instinctively knew were not always right yet we did them anyway. As a result, this caused us to stumble and fall.

I have discovered that before God allows any of His children to fall there are many opportunities for repentance. God sends us warnings. He uses people, songs, His Word, and whatever is necessary to get us to repent and turn to Him. Even after we have fallen, God is still available to help us pick up the pieces of our lives. Although the fall was not by His design, He uses what the enemy means for evil and turns it for our good (Genesis 50:20). It takes persistence to keep moving forward after you have fallen especially when the end result does not look good. It takes persistence to rise from the ashes of your life and decide that life is still worth living. God will enable you to stand and face whatever is before you. He will fill you with strength as you repent and submit to His help and leadership.

Hebrews 12:1-2 tells us that since we have such a great cloud of witnesses surrounding us, to lay aside every weight and the sin that so easily ensnares us, and run with endurance the race that lies before us, keeping our eyes on Jesus, the source and perfecter of our faith, who for the joy that lay before Him endured the cross and despised the shame, and has sat down at the right hand of God's throne. God is telling us that people are watching us as we race toward the finish line. They are watching to see who will stay the course and run the race with great endurance no matter the difficulties. Being focused on the prize is what keeps us in the race. Why are you running? What are you hoping to achieve? Once you determine the purpose of your race and the outcome you want, the race then becomes meaningful and worth fighting for.

We are running this race to be pleasing to the One we serve, Jesus. You will stay in the race and keep persisting when your eyes and your focus are steadfastly on Him. This tells me that when our focus is not on Jesus, we can be more easily tripped up by the enemy. How many of you have encountered times when you were doing well, and then the enemy attacked your mind with all types of vain imaginations? Think about this, you were minding your own business, loving the place where you were in life, and then you began to be harassed in your mind. I have been there, and at times it gets frustrating because I have to stop and do warfare with those thoughts and cast them down when all I want to do is rest and be at peace. The key is not to take ownership of the thoughts, they are not yours. 2 Corinthians 10 tells us these thoughts are vain imaginations trying to exalt themselves against the knowledge of God. We must keep Jesus in our focus at all times to annihilate these attacks by the enemy. With that said, it does not mean that the enemy will not try his best to stop you, but He who is for you is greater than any enemy who comes against you. We must keep Jesus in the center of our lives so we can always catch a glimpse of Him as we come under attack. Have you noticed that when something is center stage, no matter in which direction you turn, you will always catch a glimpse of it? This is why it is so vital to keep Jesus in the center of your life so He is always in your view.

Capture those negative, harmful thoughts by speaking the Word of God and nullifying the devil's attacks.

Remember, Jesus defeated him in the wilderness by the power of God's Word, and so can you. Send the unwholesome thoughts back to the devil, and remind Him you are the righteousness of God in Christ Jesus (2 Corinthian 5:21). You must continue to persist against all odds if you really want to attain the victory.

Persistence must become a part of your daily life. You have to persist when praying and while studying the Word. The enemy will try to bombard your mind with negative thoughts that are designed to break your focus and keep you away from your prayer time with God but remember that the One you are praying to wants an audience with you so He can help you. You are not wasting your time when you persist in prayer. Your persistence will pay off because you will connect with Jesus who wants to have intimate fellowship with you.

Philippians 3:12-14 says not that I have already obtained all this, or have already arrived at my goal, but I press on to take hold of that for which Christ Jesus took hold of me. Brothers and sisters, I do not consider myself yet to have taken hold of it. But one thing I do: Forgetting what is behind and straining toward what is ahead, I press on toward the goal to win the prize for which God has called me heavenward in Christ Jesus. Let's explore some wisdom tips in this passage. You persist because the goal is worth attaining. You are not persisting because you have already reached the goal; you are persisting because the goal is still in front of you. The reason for your persistence is because Jesus has pursued you and captured your heart. Our pursuit of Jesus is not one-sided. He first pursued us and this is the reason we have fellowship with Him, the

Father, and the Holy Spirit. I have discovered that Jesus' pursuit of us is not a one-time event; He continues to pursue us throughout our journey of life because He loves to fellowship with us.

When you let go of the difficulties of your past it is easier for you to connect to God in prayer. Sometimes it is hard to pray because the enemy reminds us of some former failures that make us feel unworthy. This is his attempt to keep you away from the One who can bring you to a place of peace. If the last sin you committed caused you to feel that there is no point in praying because you have messed up so badly, then the enemy is winning. He is interrupting your communion with the Savior because of feelings of shame and unworthiness. Jesus knows we will fall short of His standards at times and this is the reason He has given us an escape when we sin. 1 John 1:9 says if we confess our sin He is faithful and just to forgive us and to cleanse us from all unrighteousness. Since He cannot lie, you can rest assured that when you are sincerely sorry, you will receive forgiveness.

I challenge and encourage you not to let disobedience, lack of faith, lack of persistence, or anything else cause you to miss out on a deep, intimate prayer life. Prayer is the foundation for everything in your life. It is the glue that holds it all together and is the way to find peace in the midst of the storms. It is your sustainer during seasons of sickness and your hope line as you wait for your financial circumstances to change. Prayer is how you gain success and keep living in victory. It strengthens and anchors you.

God's Son, Jesus, also prayed because He understood that connecting with the Father and maintaining that connection was vital to His well-being. The same is true for you as well. God hears your prayers! He will answer you and come to your rescue if you do not stop seeking Him. I pray you experience release from anxiety and stress as you connect with the One who has the answers for your life.

PRAYERS THAT PRODUCE RESULTS

**"In order for your prayers to produce the results you
seek, you must make sure you are praying in accordance with God's will."**

Is it your deepest desire to see results in your life
when you pray? Do you want to change your circumstances for the better? Then the answer is prayer! I
can say conclusively that your prayers will produce results
that will change YOU. I am a firm believer that Jesus does
not waste a single thing that has ever happened to us. We
are told in Romans 8:28 that all things work together for
good to them that love God, to them who are called
according to His purposes. The key to having all the difficult circumstances in your life, working in your favor, is to
love God. God ensures that any evil thing that has
happened to you works out for your good. I have discovered through the Word and also by watching God work in
peoples' lives, that He never allows the enemy to have ultimate victory over His children. I often share this statement

when I teach the Word, "God will take you back to where the enemy thought he defeated you, and often gives you victory over him in the same place, and at times, in front of some of the same people who witnessed your previous defeat. The enemy will never have total victory in your life. He may win a few battles but will never win the war." God will never allow your foe to have the last say in your life and triumph over you. Prayer is a powerful key to your success over the enemy. When you lay the foundation of any venture with prayer, God will move on your behalf.

In order for your prayers to produce the results you seek, you must make sure you are praying in accordance with God's will. What is His will? His will for us is written in the pages of His Word. So to know His will for you, you must get to know His Word. Knowing His Word will help you pray effectively. As I previously shared, Isaiah 55:11 tells us that He sends His Word out and it shall not return to Him void, but must accomplish what He pleases and prosper where He sends it. This then is your answer. You are promised that when you declare the Word, when you send it out, it cannot return empty to your life but it will produce the desired results. It will return a harvest to you and help you attain the victory you are seeking.

The reason some people do not see the results of their prayers is because they pray their emotions and frustrations, and not the Word of God. God will not answer us when we are praying out of anger and frustration because we are not praying in faith. Often when we pray this way, we are mad that God has not yet moved in our situations. Can anyone attest to this? I can. Frustrated prayers say we don't trust God. While frustrated, we may be thinking why bother to pray, God does not hear me anyway. We pray but we don't necessarily believe that God is going to move this time either, since He did not move the other times we prayed. We just go through the motions and our prayers seem to be bouncing off the ceiling. The Word tells us very clearly that when we pray we must believe that we have received the petitions we desire from God, at the time we actually pray. Numbers 23:19 tells us that God is not a man that He should lie, nor the son of man that He should repent. Has He not said it and will He not do it? Do you hear what the Word is telling you? God cannot lie, if He has given you His word/promises, He has obligated Himself to make it good. So instead of praying out of frustration, find the promises in His Word that pertain to your situation, and go to Him in faith declaring what His Word says then wait on Him to move. He will move! Prayer is the foundation you lay continually that will generate the right harvest in every season of your life.

A few years ago, I had one of those moments where I felt that all the hard work, prayers, and laboring that my team and I had done for the Lord, were not producing the results for which we were praying. In the midst of this frustrating time, I was driving along a freeway and saw a massive building being built. I clearly heard the voice of the Holy Spirit whisper these words in my ears, "Do you see how tall that building is? The foundation has to be just as deep as the height of the building to sustain it. When the rains and storms come, it will not topple over because the foundation runs deep. The same thing applies to you and the vision I have given you. Through the waiting, I am laying a VERY deep foundation on which you can build something lasting on. What you have built through prayer and while waiting, will be sustained during the storms because it is built on the right foundation of trusting in My faithfulness." I discovered that my frustration stemmed from not realizing that God is faithful no matter how long the journey. He will accomplish His plans through me. The only way for me to miss doing the work He wants to accomplish with my life is if I abort His vision in the midst of my doubt and frustration. To remain steady in the waiting, I MUST continue to pray until the breakthrough comes.

In this chapter, I want to give you some assurances of what God's Word can produce in your life if you will simply do what Jesus did—pray continually using the Word. When Jesus was tempted by the devil in the wilderness, He used the Word of God to soundly defeat His opponent. You will defeat the enemy and get the victory the same way Jesus did by declaring the Word of God. We are told numerous times in the Word that the name of God is powerful, and it is. Yet Psalm 138:2 tells us that He has magnified His Word above all His name. This tells me there is power in the Word of God which is released as we declare it over every situation we face. We are also told in Matthew 24:35 that heaven and earth will pass away, but His words will never pass away. Once again, we see the significance of the Word. When we pray the Word, we are praying in accordance with God's will. His Word will bring the right results in your life and give you the harvest you desire.

I have discovered that there is a scripture for every single situation we may face. God's Word is the antidote for every trial. We, however, are responsible for finding scriptures and praying them over our circumstances and through all the difficult seasons of life.

As I conclude this book, I am including some sample prayers that are filled with the Word of God. I know these prayers will produce a huge harvest of blessings in the life of every person who will dare to pray God's Word over their situation. I encourage you to develop your own prayers using these sample prayers. As you pray His Word, may you be encouraged to trust God, and to believe that His Word will not return to you empty but will bring peace, hope, and stability to your life, in Jesus' name.

Praying the Word of God = RESULTS:

PRAYER FOR PEACE

Father, in the name of Jesus, I, (*your name*), thank You that the peace of God is operating fully in my life. I thank You that *Psalm 27:13-14* assures me that I will see the goodness of the Lord in my life. It also tells me that if I wait on the Lord and am courageous my heart will become strong. I thank You that *Psalm 29:11* says, You will give me strength and You will bless me with peace. Father, as I put my hope in You, *Psalm 38:15* says, You will hear me. Father, if there is anyone who has anything against me, then I thank You that *Psalm 55:18* says that You will redeem me from every battle, unharmed. I thank You for Your promise of protection.

Father, I choose to have a joyful heart and I thank You that *Proverbs 17:22* says that when I have a joyful heart it is medicine to my whole body. I choose Your joy in all areas of my life. Father, when I am afraid, I can rest in *Psalm 56:3-4* which states that when I am afraid, I can trust in You, in God, whose word I praise, in God I trust, I will not fear, what can man do to me? Holy One, I thank You for *Philippians 4:7* which says Your supernatural peace which passes all understanding will guard and keep my heart and mind in Christ Jesus, in Jesus name I pray.

PRAYER for My Family

Father, I thank You that my family is in Your hands, and based on *John 10:28-29,* no one can pluck them out of Your hands. I thank You that You are watching over them and taking care of every need they have. I receive *Psalm 28:7* which says that the Lord is my strength and my shield and my heart can trust in Him concerning my family. Father, I commit to do what *Psalm 121:1-2* tells me to do, so I raise my eyes toward the mountains where my help comes from because my help comes from the Lord, the Maker of heaven and earth. You are my only hope and help. I trust You to meet the needs of my family, in Jesus' name.

I thank You that based on *Psalm 138:8,* You will fulfill Your purposes for me and my family. Lord, I thank You that Your love is eternal, and You do not abandon the work of Your hands toward my family. I also thank You that *Psalm 145:18* says, You are near to all who call out to You, so I thank You for answering me when I call to You on behalf of the needs in my family, in Jesus' name.

Prayer for My Spouse

Father, You tell us in the Word to pray for one another. I come to you today, on behalf of my spouse, asking you to bless and keep (*their name*) safe. *Ecclesiastes 4:12* tells me that although one may be overpowered, two can defend themselves. A cord of three strands is not quickly broken." I stand on the promise of Your Word that the enemy will not be able to destroy this union You have put together. *Mark 10:9* says what God has joined together, let no one separate. I agree with the scripture that nothing will ever be able to separate us, in Jesus' name. Teach me how to enjoy each day with my spouse all the days of the life that God has given us under the sun based on *Ecclesiastes 9:9.*

1 Peter 4:8 tells us to love each other deeply because love covers a multitude of sins. Help us to love each other deeply so we can see only the good qualities that you have placed in us. Help us to deal humbly and gently with each other. Teach us how to be patient, bearing with one another in love. Help us to make every effort to keep the unity of the spirit through the bond of peace as we are told in *Ephesians 4:2-3. Ephesians 4:32* tells us to be kind to one another, tenderhearted, forgiving one another, even as God in Christ forgave us. Teach us how to live these words out daily, and to forgive each other quickly.

FATHER, remind us of *1 Corinthians 10:13* which says, "No temptation has overtaken us except what is common to man; but God *is* faithful, who will not allow us to be tempted beyond what we are able to handle, but with the temptation God will show us the way of escape." Teach us how to hold our marriage in the highest honor and keep our marriage bed pure. Help us not to do anything that will dishonor our marriage. Based on *Hebrews 13:4*, God will judge the adulterer and all the sexually immoral. Father, we trust in the Lord above all else to keep us from the plots of the enemy to destroy our marriage.

Teach us Father how to love like You love. Remind us of *1 John 4:7-8* which says, "Beloved, let us love one another, for love is from God, and whoever loves has been born of God and knows God. Anyone who does not love does not know God, because God is love." Give us this divine love for one another, in Jesus' name. When we face difficulties remind us of *Joshua 1:9* which says, "Be strong and coura-geous; do not be frightened or dismayed, for the Lord your God is with you wherever you go.

As we trust in You, we acknowledge You will be with us each day of our marriage, and we pledge to put You in the center of our marriage. Remind us daily that with You in the center, we will always be able to catch a glimpse of You, no matter in which direction we turn. Thank You for choosing us for each other. We desire to glorify You and advance Your kingdom on earth as it is in heaven through our marriage, In Jesus' name.

Prayer for My Children

Father, I thank You that I have obedient children. *Psalm 37:26* says the seed of the righteous is blessed and therefore my children are blessed. *Psalm 28:7* declares that the Lord is my strength and my shield, my heart trusts in Him, and I am helped. Thank You that You have given me the strength to provide for my children and to be a shield around them. I thank You that *1 King 17:13* tells me not to be afraid but to do as You say and You will bless my efforts. I know You will bless my efforts on behalf of my children. *Psalm 37:5* tells me to commit my ways to the Lord and to trust also in Him and He will act. Father, I commit my children to You, and I trust You knowing You will do what is best for them.

I thank You Father that *Psalm 40:5* says that You have done many things, Your wonderful works and Your plans for us are great and none can compare with You. You have indeed done wonderful works in my children, and I thank You. I thank You, Father, that *Luke 1:37* says that nothing will be impossible with God, so I claim this promise for my children. You will prosper and bless them with long healthy lives, in Jesus' name.

Prayer for Healing

Father, in the name of Jesus, I, (*your name*), thank You that You have blessed me with good health. *Exodus 15:26* tells me that if I carefully follow the Lord my God and obey Him, He will not bring any sickness on me for He is the Lord who heals me. Father, *Exodus 23:25* says that if I worship the Lord my God He will bless me and take away sickness and disease from me. I thank You that *Deuteronomy 7:15* says that the Lord will remove all sickness from me and I believe and receive Your Word. I also thank You that *Psalm 91:16* promises me that with a long (healthy) life will You satisfy me and show me Your salvation.

I take *Psalm 107:20* as my personal promise that You sent Your Word and healed me and removed me from the pit. I thank You that *Proverbs 4:20-23* tells me that if I keep Your Words within my heart and not lose sight of them, that they will be life to me and health to my whole body. Father, I thank You so much that *Jeremiah 1:12* says You hasten to fulfill Your Word in my life. Based on *Isaiah 53:4,* You bore my sicknesses and diseases and carried my pain, and by Your wounds, I am totally healed and made whole. I thank You that *Mark 11:23* says that if I speak to the mountains in my life they must move. So I speak to the mountains of sickness and disease and command them to move. Sickness and disease have no power over me, in Jesus' name.

PRAYER FOR EMOTIONAL Struggles

Father, in the name of Jesus, I, (*your name*), seek You today for help with the emotional turmoil that I am feeling. *Philippians 4:6-7* tells me, "Do not be anxious about anything but in everything by prayer and petition, with thanksgiving, to make my requests known to You and the peace of God that passes all understanding will guard my heart and mind in Christ Jesus. Jesus, please help me not to be overcome with the emotions that are attempting to drown me.

Colossians 3:2 tells me to set my mind on things above not on the things that are on earth. Holy Spirit, help me to focus on You and not on the difficult circumstances in and around me.

Romans 8:6 tells me that the mind set on the flesh is death, but the mind set on the Spirit is life and peace. I fix my mind, heart, and emotions on You today and ask You to please steady me. *1 Peter 5:7* tells me to cast every burden and care on You because You care for me. *Matthew 11:28-30* invites me to come to You because I am weary and laden down with cares, and it tells me Your yoke is easy and Your burden is light. I give You my burdens and make a decision to yoke myself to You so I can survive this turmoil.

2 Corinthians 10:5 tells me to cast down every vain imagination, and every high thing that exalts itself against the knowledge of God, and to bring into captivity every thought to the obedience of Christ. Jesus, please help me to control the wayward thoughts that are running through my mind. *Romans 1:17* tells me that the righteous man shall live by faith. I have anchored my faith in You. Allow Your power to flood my emotions, and bring healing and deliverance to my life.

Proverbs 3:5-6 reminds me to trust in the Lord with all my heart and to not lean on my own understanding. It tells me to trust You in all my ways and You will direct my path. Help me to do this today so I can experience your peace, in Jesus' name.

Prayer for Singleness

Prayer for Singleness Father, as a single person I, (your name), ask You to help me to focus my heart on You as I wait on You to manifest Your plans and purposes for my life. Matthew 6:33 tells me to seek first the kingdom of God and His righteousness and all these things will be given to me as well. Father, I choose to seek after You and to make a difference for You, while I wait on You to bring me the right spouse at the proper time. 1 Corinthians 7:34 tells me that while I am unmarried I am more concerned about the Lord's affairs and that I can be devoted to the Lord in both body and spirit. Teach me how to rest in You knowing You are faithful to Your promises. Galatians 4:27 says to rejoice, barren woman who does not bear; break forth and shout, you who are not in labor; for more numerous are the children of the desolate than of the one who has a husband. Thank You that I can rejoice because God is for me in the midst of my waiting. Hebrews 4:15 tells me Jesus understands where I am. It says, "For we do not have a high priest who is unable to sympathize with our weakness, but one who in every respect has been tempted as we are, yet without sin." Jesus was single and understands where I am in my singleness, so I can talk to Him about it and He will hear and answer me. Jeremiah 31:3 says, "I have loved you with an everlasting love, therefore I have continued my faithfulness to you." Help me to remember that when others are unfaithful, You are always faithful to me. You hear my prayers and will move on my behalf.

Help me Father to be successful in my singleness so I will have great success in my marriage. Father, You tell me in Haggai 2:23 that You will make me like Your signet ring, for You have chosen me. I believe and receive it. Isaiah 43:4 says I am precious and honored in Your sight. Thank You, Father, for seeing me as special. Isaiah 49:16 tells me You have engraved me on the palms of Your hands, which tells me how special I am to You. Jeremiah 29:11 tells me You have a plan for my life and it is good and not evil. Jeremiah 1:5 says before You formed me in the womb You knew me. Since You know me, I know You have my life in total control. Help me Lord to remember this and not to settle for less than the very best You have for me, in Jesus' name.

Prayer against Demonic Attacks

Father, in the name of Jesus, I pray against every attack of the enemy that is affecting my life. *Matthew 18:18* says that what I bind on earth shall be bound in heaven, and whatsoever I loose on earth shall be loosed in heaven. I bind every attack that is staged against me, and I call them null and void in Jesus' name. I am told in *Isaiah 54:17* that no weapon that is formed against me shall prosper. I hold tightly to that promise today as I battle against the attacks of the enemy. *Isaiah 59:19* says when the enemy comes in like a flood the Spirit of the Lord will lift up a standard against Him. I ask You to fight for me.

Thank You for the seven-piece armor You have given to Believers in *Ephesians 6:14-17.* I dress myself in that armor by asking You to help me to girt myself with the belt of truth. I put on the breastplate of righteousness; and my feet are fitted with the readiness of the gospel of peace. I take the shield of faith so I can quench all the fiery darts of the wicked one. I put on the helmet of salvation to guard my mind against all the attacks of the enemy. I take the sword of the Spirit which is the Word of God; and I am praying at all times, in Jesus' name. I dress myself daily in this armor so the enemy cannot destroy me or the good work You started in me. *Ephesians 6:12* says that we do not battle against flesh and blood, but against principalities, against powers, against the rulers of the darkness of this age, against spiritual *hosts* of wickedness in heavenly *places.* Jesus, I know You soundly defeated the enemy; therefore, I have victory through You.

1 Corinthians 15:58 – tells me to be steadfast, immovable, always abounding in the work of the Lord, forasmuch as I know that my labor is not in vain the Lord. I will win over the attacks of the enemy in my life because of my steadfast hope in You. Jesus, remind me daily You defeated the enemy and that a defeated enemy has no power over me nor can he ultimately defeat me. I *John 4:4* tells me that greater is He that is in me, than he that is in the world. I thank You that You arm me with strength on a daily basis and make my way prosperous. I will be victorious over the enemy each and every day of my life.

Thank You Jesus that *Revelation 12:11* tells me that I overcome him (the devil) by the blood of the lamb and the word of my testimony. I overcome every attack today by the precious blood of Jesus. In His name alone. Amen.

Prayer for Wisdom and Favor

Father, I, (*your name*) seek You for wisdom in all areas of my life. *Proverbs 8:33-35* says that I should listen to instructions and be wise, and that if I listen to wisdom I will be happy because wisdom will be watching at my doors each day. Thank You that when I find wisdom, I find life and obtain favor from the Lord. Father, *Proverbs 8:1* says that wisdom calls out to me, and that wisdom is better than precious stones and nothing desirable can compare with her. It says, "I, wisdom share a home with shrewdness and have knowledge and discretion." I ask You, Father, to help me share my heart with wisdom.

Father, I thank You that *John 14:14* says that if I ask anything in Your name You will do it, so I ask You today to fill me with wisdom in every decision I make, in Jesus' name. I thank You, Lord that *Proverbs 16:3* says for me to commit my ways to You and all my plans will succeed. Father, *Psalm 50:15* says that when I call to You in the day of trouble, You will rescue me and You will honor me. I call to You today and ask You to fill me with wisdom and to rescue me from all fiery trials, in Jesus' name.

Prayer for My Finances

Father, it is Your greatest desire to bless me, therefore, I confess Your Word over my financial situation. I thank You that *1 Corinthians 2:9* says, "No eye has seen, no ear has heard what God has prepared for me because You love me."

Father, *John 15:7* says that if I remain in You and Your Words remain in me I can ask whatever I will and it will be done for me, therefore, Father, I ask You for an outpouring of Your financial blessings in my life. Father, *Luke 11:9-10* says to ask and it will be given to me, seek and I will find, knock and the door will be opened to me, for when I ask I will receive, and when I knock the door will be opened. I am asking, seeking, and knocking, and need You to open the door and pour finances into my life.

Father, *Proverbs 22:4* says that when I have humility and the fear of the Lord, wealth, honor, and long life will be given to me. *Matthew 6:8* says You know what I have need of before I ask, so I thank You for supplying my needs, in Jesus' name. Father, *Malachi 3:10–11* tells me that You, the Lord, says to bring all the tithe into the storehouse so that there will be food in Your house. Then it tells me to see if You will not open the floodgates of heaven and pour me out blessings that I will not have room enough to receive. It also says You will rebuke the devourer for my sake. So, as I do what You command, I thank You for providing my every need. *Luke 6:38* says to give and it will be given to me good measure, pressed down, shaken together, and running over will men give into my bosom, for with the same measure that I give out it will be measured to me again. Father, I am giving, therefore I agree, receive, and stand firm on Your promises today for my financial blessings, in Jesus' name.

PRAYER FOR MY JOB/CAREER

Father, in the name of Jesus, I, (*your name*), need a job, so thank You for the new position You have prepared for me. *Psalm 1:3* says I am like a tree planted by the rivers of water that yield its fruit in season, that my leaf shall not wither and whatsoever I do shall prosper. *Psalm 2:8* says for me to ask You and You will make the nations my inheritance and the ends of the earth my possession, therefore, I thank You that You have hand-selected the right job or position for me. I confess *Romans 4:20* which says that I do not waver in unbelief at God's promise, but am strengthened in my faith and will give glory to God for all the good things He will do in my life.

I am encouraged by *Mark 11:24* which says I must believe I have received all the things I pray and ask for, and I will have them. I thank You for the great job or promotion You are bringing into my life, and You will go beyond what I can think or imagine. Father, *Psalm 18:32* says You clothe me with strength and make my way perfect. I thank You based on Your word in *Psalm 20:4*, You will give me the desires of my heart and fulfill Your purposes in me.

Psalm 31:15 says that the course of my life is in Your power, and *Psalm 37:5* says if I commit my ways to You and trust also in You, then You will act and bring it to pass in my life. You have given me a great promise in *Proverbs 10:22* that the blessing of the Lord brings wealth, and He adds no trouble to it.

Father, Jesus said in *John 11:40*, "Didn't I tell you that if you believed you would see the glory of God?" So I thank

You that I am a believer and that I will see the glory of God in all areas of my life, especially with the right job. *Luke 1:37* reminds me that nothing is impossible for You. I also thank You that *Psalm 25:3a* says, not one person who waits on You will be disgraced. I take Your word as my medicine and wait with expectancy for their fulfillment in my life, in Jesus' name!

Prayer for My Heart's Desire

Father, thank You that I (*your name*) am called by Your name and am destined for a purpose. I thank You that *Psalm 37:4* says that if I delight myself in the Lord, He will give me the desires of my heart. Lord, I delight in Your plans for my life and the gifts You have in store for me. Father, *Psalm 1:3* also says that I am like a tree planted beside streams of water that bears its fruit in season and whose leaf does not wither, and whatsoever I, (*your name*), do shall prosper. Based on *Romans 4:20,* I thank You that like Abraham I will not waver in unbelief at Your promises, but will be strengthened in my faith and give glory to You, God, because You will provide the right opportunities for me at the right time.

Father, based on *Proverbs 3:3, 5 & 6,* I, (*your name*), will not let loyalty and faithfulness leave me. I will tie them around my neck and write them on the tablets of my heart. I make a firm decision to always trust in You, Lord, with all my heart and lean not to my own understanding; in all my ways I will acknowledge You and You will direct my path. Father, *1 Kings 8:24* says that You kept what You promised to Your servant David. You spoke directly to him and fulfilled Your promises to him. I thank You that in the same way, You will fulfill Your plans, purposes, and promises to me also, just as You did for David. And Father, I thank You for favor in my going out and coming in, and for giving me favor with men and women all around the world, in Jesus' name.

Prayer for God's **Plan for My Life and Future**

Father, I thank You that *Jeremiah 29:11* says I know the plans I have for you declares the Lord, plans to bless you and to prosper you and to give you hope and a future. Father, I thank You that *Romans 8:28* says that You will work all things together for my good because You love me and I am called according to Your purposes. It also says in *Mark 10:27* that with men it is impossible but with God, all things are possible for my life. Now Father, I know Your Word produces results, so I pray these scriptures and believe You to unfold Your plans in my life.

Mark 11:22–24 gives me a promise for the plans You have for my life. Thank You that it says to have faith in God; "I assure you, (*your name*), if you say to this mountain be lifted up and thrown into the sea and do not doubt in your heart but believe what you say, it will happen for you. Therefore, I tell you, (*your name*), that whatever things you pray for believe that you receive them and you shall have them." I also see in *John 4:34* where it says that my food is to do the will of Him who sent me and to finish His work. So, Father, I desire to do the work that You have assigned me and to walk in the fullness of the plans that You have for my life, in Jesus' name.

Prayer for Fulfilling My Destiny

Father, in the name of Jesus, I thank You that You order my steps daily. *Psalm 37:5, 23* says if I commit my ways to the Lord and trust in Him, He will bring it to pass. I also thank You that this same passage says that a man's steps are established by the Lord and He takes pleasure in his way. I thank You for taking pleasure in me and for establishing every step I take. Father, I thank You that *Psalm 85:13* says that righteousness will go before me and prepare the way for my steps. And *Psalm 119:35, 105 & 133* say, You help me to stay on the path because You take pleasure in me, and that Your Word is a lamp unto my feet and a light unto my path. Thank You for establishing me and making my steps steady. Your promises for my life are yes and amen.

Proverbs 3:5-7 says that I must trust in the Lord with all my heart and lean not on my own understanding, but in all my ways to acknowledge Him and He will direct my paths. I see in *Psalm 5:3* that at daybreak You will hear my voice, therefore at daybreak, I plead my case to You and then watch expectantly for You to act. I know that You have heard me and that You will act according to Your good pleasure for my life. I thank You that *Proverbs 16:7* says that because my ways please You, that You will make even my enemies be at peace with me, so I thank You for favor with men, women, children, leaders, and even my enemies. Father, You said in *Isaiah 61:8* that You love justice and that

You will faithfully reward me and make an everlasting covenant with me. Thank You that You have established a covenant with me and You plan to use me for Your highest glory and honor. Father, I pray *Psalm 27:11*, that You show me Your way Lord, and lead me on a level path. I thank You for opening all the doors that only You can open for me and closing the ones You have not ordained to be opened in my life, in Jesus' name.

PRAYER FOR INTEGRITY in My Life

Father, in the name of Jesus, I ask You to fulfill my desire to help others and be a blessing to them. *Mark 4:24* says that if I pay attention to what I hear everything will be measured and added to my life. Father, just as Abraham believed You and it was credited to him for righteousness, so *Galatians 3:6* says You credit me with the ability through Your righteousness to provide aid to others when You present their needs to me. Your Word promises in *Psalm 84:11* that You will give me grace and glory and You do not withhold anything good from those who live in integrity. *Proverbs 28:18* says whoever walks in integrity will be delivered, but he who is crooked in his ways will suddenly fall. *Proverbs 2:20-21* also says that by Your wisdom, discretion, and understanding we will walk in the way of the good and keep to the paths of the righteous; for the upright will inhabit the land, and those with integrity will remain in it.

Thank You that I am a person of integrity who will do for others what You have instructed me to do. I thank You that You have taught me to live like *Philippians 4:11*, being content in whatever circumstance I find myself. I thank You that *Colossians 3:23* says that whatever I do, to do it enthusiastically as something done for the Lord and not men. Help me to be enthusiastic about helping others find their position in You. I thank You, Father, that *Psalm 102:13* says that You will arise and have compassion on Zion (*your name*) for it is time to show favor to her, the appointed time has come. I stand in the place of Zion, and I take this promise for my life and loved ones. I thank You that Your favor and integrity will begin to abound in my life and flood and overtake me, in Jesus' name.

PRAYER FOR MAKING RIGHT, **Godly Decisions**

Father, it is my sincere desire to make good and wholesome decisions. Thank You that *Psalm 34:4* says that I sought the Lord and He answered me and delivered me from all my fears. *Proverbs 12:1* tells me that if I love instruction then I will love knowledge. Father, I choose to receive Your instructions concerning the way I should live my life. I follow the guideline found in *Ephesians 6:7,* which tells me to render service with a good attitude as to the Lord and not to man. *Psalm 86:7* says that when I call on You in the day of my distress, You will answer me. I thank You for answering me as I call to You for directions, and as I make decisions. *Philippians 1:6* clearly says, "I am sure of this, that He who started a good work in me will carry it on to completion until the day of Christ Jesus."

Father, *Proverbs 3:5-6* tells me to trust in the LORD with all my heart; and lean not on my own understanding. In all my ways to acknowledge Him, and He shall direct my paths. *Jeremiah 29:11* says For I know the thoughts that I think toward you, says the LORD, thoughts of peace, and not of evil, to give you an expected end. I see in *James 1:5-6* that if I lack wisdom, I should ask God, who gives generously to all without finding fault, and it will be given to me. But when I ask, I must believe and not doubt, because the one who doubts is like a wave of the sea, blown and tossed by the wind. I am asking You now to please help me to lean on You daily and trust You for wisdom.

Proverbs 11:14 says where there is no guidance, people fall, but in an abundance of counselors there is safety. *1 John 5:14-15* says this is the confidence that we have toward Him, that if we ask anything according to His will He hears us, and if we know that He hears us, He will give us the desires of our heart. Please help me to always make the right decisions. Thank You that *1 Thessalonians 5:17-18* says for me to pray constantly and give thanks in everything for this is God's will for me in Christ Jesus. I thank You that each day You will order my steps and help me to make godly decisions, in Jesus' name!

PRAYER FOR FREEDOM FROM FEAR, **Worry, and Anxiety**

Father, I thank You that I, (*your name*) have freedom in You because of Your Son, Jesus Christ. Thank You for Your freedom from anxiety and worry. I acknowledge that those things are not from You and I will not give any place to the enemy to cause stress in my life. Therefore, I declare Your Word over myself and I know that You will free me from all of life's concerns because my hope is in You. As I pray these scriptures over myself, I stand on Isaiah 55:11 which says that Your Word shall not return to You empty, but it shall accomplish what You please and prosper where You send it. So Father I declare these scriptural promises over my life in Jesus' name:

- *Deuteronomy 31:6* – "Be strong and courageous. Do not be afraid or terrified because of them, for the LORD your God goes with you; he will never leave you nor forsake you."
- *Proverbs 12:25* – "Anxiety in a man's heart weighs him down, but a good word makes him glad."
- *Proverbs 17:22* – "A joyful heart is good medicine, but a crushed spirit dries up the bones."
- *Psalm 34:4* – "I sought the LORD, and he answered me and delivered me from all my fears."
- *Psalm 27:1* – "The LORD is my light and my salvation whom shall I fear? The Lord is the stronghold of my life of whom shall I be afraid?"
- *Psalm 37:5* – "Commit your way to the LORD; trust in him, and he will act."
- *Psalm 56:3-4* – "When I am afraid, I will trust in you. In God, whose word I praise, in God I trust; I will not be afraid. What can mortal man do to me?"
- *Proverbs 3:5-6* – "Trust in the LORD with all your heart, and do not lean on your own understanding. In all your ways acknowledge him, and he will make straight your paths."

- *Isaiah 41:10* – "So do not fear, for I am with you; do not be dismayed, for I am your God. I will strengthen you and help you; I will uphold you with my righteous right hand."
- *Philippians 4:6-7* - "Do not be anxious about anything, but in everything by prayer and supplication with thanksgiving, let your requests be made known to God. And the peace of God, which surpasses all understanding, will guard your hearts and your minds in Christ Jesus."
- *1 Peter 5:6-7* – "Humble yourselves, therefore, under the mighty hand of God so that at the proper time he may exalt you, casting all your anxieties on him, because he cares for you."
- *Hebrews 13:6* – "So we can confidently say, 'The Lord is my helper; I will not fear; what can man do to me?'"
- *Psalms 94:19* – "When the cares of my heart are many, your consolations cheer my soul."
- *Romans 8:28* – "And we know that for those who love God, all things work together for good, for those who are called according to his purpose."
- *Philippians 4:13* – "I can do all things through Christ which strengtheneth me."
- *Philippians 4:19* – "And my God will supply every need of yours according to his riches in glory in Christ Jesus."
- *Matthew 6:26* – "Look at the birds of the air: they neither sow nor reap nor gather into barns, and yet your heavenly Father feeds them. Are you not much better than they?"

- *Matthew 6:34* – "Therefore do not be anxious about tomorrow, for tomorrow will be anxious for itself. Sufficient for the day is its own trouble."
- *2 Corinthians 4:17* – "For this light momentary affliction is preparing for us an eternal weight of glory beyond all comparison."
- *Revelation 21:4* – "He will wipe away every tear from their eyes, and death shall be no more, neither shall there be mourning, nor crying, nor pain anymore, for the former things have passed away."

Thank You, Lord, for hearing and answering my prayer, and for freeing me from fear, worry, and anxiety, in Jesus' name.

PRAYER **for the Nations**

Father, I come to You in the name of Jesus, and remind You of what You said in *2 Chronicles 7:14*, if my people, who are called by my name, will humble themselves and pray and seek my face and turn from their wicked ways, then I will hear from heaven, and I will forgive their sin and will heal their land. We are crying out for the healing we need in the nations of the world. Your Word says in *Proverbs 14:34* that righteousness exalts a nation, so we are calling out to You for righteousness to begin to flood this nation and then spread around the world. Father, You declare in *Isaiah 59:19* that when the enemy shall come in like a flood, the Spirit of the LORD shall lift up a standard against him. We are praying for those in the nations who are experiencing fear because of disasters and tragic events, and we declare that *2 Timothy 1:7* says you have not given us a spirit of fear but of power, love, and a sound mind.

Father, You alone are the nation's fortress and salvation, therefore we will never be shaken when disaster comes. You said in *Psalm 33:12* that blessed is the nation whose God is the Lord, and the people whom He has chosen as His heritage. We want to be the nation that crowns You Lord over us. *In Psalm 2:8,* You said to ask and You will make the nations our inheritance, so we are praying that You turn the nations back to You because only You can rule over them righteously and with justice.

We ask You to give strength to the people in the nations and bless them with Your peace. Based on *Zechariah 4:6,* we acknowledge the changes that need to take place in the nations will not be by might, nor by power, but by the Spirit of the Lord. You said we can decree a thing and it is so, so we decree that all the prayers that have been prayed will cause changes in the nations of the world, in Jesus' name. Thank you Lord, Amen and so be it!

I declare that as we begin to pray these prayers over ourselves, our children, spouses, friends, and the nations our gracious God will open to us the floodgates of heaven and pour out such blessings we will not be able to contain them. Thank You that You always hear us when we pray, in Jesus' name, Amen.

As I conclude this book, I want to remind you once again that prayer is a MUST_for every believer. It is the glue that holds you together in the midst of every trial and storm. Prayer steadies you as you journey toward the victories God has in store for your life. Embrace the gift of prayer and know assuredly God does hear you and will indeed answer you.

I pray that your prayer life has been enriched in every way after reading this book, and it continues to grow deeper and more intimate day by day. I hope each time you pray you begin to experience the power and presence of God in a deeper and richer way than ever before. May God fill you to overflowing with all you need to have a rich and fulfilling prayer life.

Remember PRAYER is not optional; it is a MUST for anyone who wants to be successful and have victory over every circumstance of life. Keep praying, your help is on the way!

AMEN – SO BE IT!

A PRAYER FOR SALVATION

"He does not love others more than He loves you."

Father, I acknowledge You sent Jesus into the world to die for my sins. I believe that He is Your Son; He was born of a virgin, and He died and rose from the dead for my sins. I acknowledge I have sinned and fallen short of Your standards, and ask You to forgive me. I invite Jesus to come into my heart because the Bible says He is the way, truth, and life, and no man comes to the Father but by Him. Father, I am coming to You in the precious name of Your Son, Jesus. I thank You for saving me and setting me free, in Jesus' name. Amen!

YOU CAN TRUST HIM

Whether you're grappling with past wounds, uncertain about your faith, or simply seeking a deeper connection with God, "You Can Trust Him" will guide you toward healing, hope, and a renewed sense of trust. Step into a life of unwavering faith and experience the transformative power of trusting in God's unchanging goodness.

HAVE **you ever been in a tough season** in your life where you had to endure some hard, difficult things? If you have, you may have discovered the key that enabled you to be victorious—perseverance. Perseverance has been the cornerstone for many who have chosen a life of faith. It is necessary to have grit to get through tough times and perseverance is that grit. Without perseverance, many of us would give up when our way is paved with difficulties. If we give up, we will miss some of the greatest opportunities to know God and His Son in a rich and powerful way. Perseverance means to abide, to endure, to persist, to remain steady in trials, and not to give up.

Pause for a moment and review these definitions. Do you see your reflection in any of these words? Have you endured your hard seasons and trying times with patience? Have you remained steady and focused when you were overcome with trials and tribulations? Have you persisted while not being sure if you had the strength to continue? Let me share a secret with you. God knew all along you had all that was necessary to be victorious over these hardships. The enemy cannot send anything into your life that God is not fully aware of, and since He knows all things, He knows what you can handle. He also knows what difficulties will develop His character in you and showcase His power through you. 1 Corinthians 15:58 is one of my favorite scriptures. It says, to be steadfast, immovable, always abounding in the work of the Lord for you know your labor is not in vain in Him. The scripture tells you to be steady; to let nothing move you; to stay the course because you are not laboring in vain.

In everything you face, God is with you and will give you a victorious end. Perseverance is not a one-time event; it must become a lifestyle. It is something you will need to do continually if you are determined to succeed. Those who persevere will succeed because they refuse to give up. Our Christian life is a race to the finish line; we are not aimlessly running around as if we have no destination in mind. In any race, the one who persists, who never gives up in the face of difficulties, will always triumph. Here is a perfect example.

A few years ago, we went to Zimbabwe to minister and to do missions. As is our usual practice, we visited a children's hospital to pray for the kids and to bless them with gifts. While we were going through the wards, I came across this little girl who was about eight years old. She went from one person to another saying hello and smiling, and was constantly singing. She seemed healthy and so very joyful. When I asked her if she knew Jesus, her answer was an instantaneous and firm, yes. I then asked her to sing a song for me and she broke out into a song that brought a smile to all of our faces. Her parents watched her with smiles but there was also sadness in their eyes. I commented that she seemed healthy and asked why she was in the hospital. She was there because one of her legs had been amputated and it had developed an infection. Throughout all her health challenges and the amputation, we were told she never lost her joy or her smile. Her spirit was infectious and contagious.

Although there were many sick children in the ward, the joy of this one small child lit up the entire place. I pondered to myself then, and even now, how often I lack joy when facing difficult seasons. It is hard at times to find a smile, much less to encourage others. This young girl was facing a lifetime of challenges in a country where so many healthy people struggle to survive, yet she embraced her difficulties by holding onto her joy. It is my hope and prayer she will always find her strength in the joy she exhibited. Nehemiah 8:10 tells us the joy of the Lord is our strength. I encourage you to find your joy in the hope that Jesus can cause you to triumph over all your troubles.

PURCHASE your copy now by clicking the link or visiting our website.

You Can TRUST Him
www.jemmuniquegifts.com

NOTES

Zondervan Bible Commentary
    FF Bruce, General Edition
    (Grandrapids, MI)

Vine's Expository Dictionary
    Edited by Stephen D. Renn
    Hendrickson Publishers Marketing LLC

ABOUT THE AUTHOR

Joan Murray is committed to helping people discover their destinies. She is the founder and CEO of Joan Murray Ministries and Seeds of Hope Worldwide Missions. Joan is dedicated to teaching, training, equipping, and helping people with various life struggles.

Joan is a minister, Bible teacher, author, and missionary. She has traveled extensively throughout the United States and internationally sharing the gospel message and serving the needs of the oppressed. Joan currently resides in Houston, Texas.

If you would like to know more about Joan Murray Ministries or Seeds of Hope Worldwide Missions, please get in touch with us at:

Joan Murray Ministries & Seeds Of Hope Worldwide
Missions
26340 FM 1736
Waller, TX 77848
281-398-2501
email: jmmcontactus@gmail.com
website: www.jemmuniquegift.com
website: www.joanmurrayministries.org

**Changing Lives Through the Power and Truth of God's
Word.**